I0813460

The Grover E. Murray Studies in the American Southwest

Also in the series

Brujerías: Stories of Witchcraft and the Supernatural in the American Southwest and Beyond, by Nasario García

Cacti of Texas: A Field Guide, by A. Michael Powell, James F. Weedin, and Shirley A. Powell

Cacti of the Trans-Pecos and Adjacent Areas, by A. Michael Powell and James F. Weedin

Cowboy Park: Steer-Roping Contests on the Border, by John O. Baxter

Dance All Night: Those Other Southwestern Swing Bands, Past and Present, by Jean A. Boyd

Deep Time and the Texas High Plains: History and Geology, by Paul H. Carlson

From Texas to San Diego in 1851: The Overland Journal of Dr. S. W. Woodhouse, Surgeon-Naturalist of the Sitgreaves Expedition, edited by Andrew Wallace and Richard H. Hevly

Grasses of South Texas: A Guide to Identification and Value, by James H. Everitt, D. Lynn Drawe, Christopher R. Little, and Robert I. Lonard

Kit Carson and the First Battle of Adobe Walls: A Tale of Two Journeys, by Alvin R. Lynn

In the Shadow of the Carmens: Afield with a Naturalist in the Northern Mexican Mountains, by Bonnie Reynolds McKinney

Javelinas: Collared Peccaries of the Southwest, by Jane Manaster

Land of Enchantment Wildflowers: A Guide to the Plants of New Mexico, by LaShara J. Nieland and Willa F. Finley

Little Big Bend: Common, Uncommon, and Rare Plants of Big Bend National Park, by Roy Morey

Lone Star Wildflowers: A Guide to Texas Flowering Plants, by LaShara J. Nieland and Willa F. Finley

My Wild Life: A Memoir of Adventures within America's National Parks, by Roland H. Wauer

Myth, Memory, and Massacre: The Pease River Capture of Cynthia Ann Parker, by Paul H. Carlson and Tom Crum

Pecans: The Story in a Nutshell, by Jane Manaster

Picturing a Different West: Vision, Illustration, and the Tradition of Austin and Cather, by Janis P. Stout

Plants of Central Texas Wetlands, by Scott B. Fleenor and Stephen Welton Taber

Seat of Empire: The Embattled Birth of Austin, Texas, by Jeffrey Stuart Kerr

Texas, New Mexico, and the Compromise of 1850: Boundary Dispute and Sectional Crisis, by Mark J. Stegmaier

Texas Quilts and Quilters: A Lone Star Legacy, by Marcia Kaylakie with Janice Whittington

Truly Texas Mexican: A Native Culinary Heritage in Recipes, by Adán Medrano

The Wineslinger Chronicles: Texas on the Vine, by Russell D. Kane

A History of the Texas Cowboys' Christmas Ball

FOREWORD BY MICHAEL MARTIN MURPHEY

Texas Tech University Press

This book is typeset in Adobe Garamond. The paper used in this book meets the minimum requirements of ANSI/NISO Z39.48-1992 (R1997). ♾

Designed by Ashley Beck
Cover photograph/illustration by Tiffany Homan

Library of Congress Cataloging-in-Publication Data
Carlson, Paul Howard.
Dancin' in Anson : a history of the Texas Cowboys' Christmas ball / Paul H. Carlson ; foreword by Michael Martin Murphey.
pages cm. — (Grover E. Murray studies in the American Southwest)
Summary: ""Explores the history and reenactment of the Texas Cowboys' Christmas Ball held in Anson, TX every year since 1934; analyzes the poem by William Lawrence Chittenden written about the Anson Christmas dances in the 1880s and is the basis for the reenactment."—Provided by publisher"— Provided by publisher.
Includes bibliographical references and index.
ISBN 978-0-89672-891-2 (hardback) — ISBN 978-0-89672-892-9 (e-book)
1. Chittenden, William Lawrence, 1862-1934—Criticism and interpretation. 2. Christmas—Texas. 3. American poetry—History and criticism. 4. West (U.S.)—In literature. I. Title.
PS1294.C3Z56 2014
811'.3—dc23 2014027986

14 15 16 17 18 19 20 21 22 / 9 8 7 6 5 4 3 2 1

Texas Tech University Press
Box 41037 | Lubbock, Texas 79409-1037 USA
800.832.4042 | ttup@ttu.edu | www.ttupress.org

For Suanne Holtman and Bernie Holtman, the heart and soul of the Modern Texas Cowboys' Christmas Ball, and in memory of Leonora Barrett and Hybernia Grace.

CONTENTS

PHOTOGRAPHS

MAPS

The Texas Cowboys' Christmas Ball in Anson, Texas, is a high-stepping, warm-hearted Wild West dance that can't be compared to anything else in the world. I've had the honor to perform at this high-spirited, family-oriented musical Christmas celebration since 1993. This pure Americana dance and party feature traditional songs and dance tunes popular in the days of the energetic frontiersmen, daring mountain men, intrepid pioneers, and boot-pounding cattle drovers, as well as contemporary country and western songs that emphasize the American ranching culture.

Texas is a proud, liberty-loving territory founded by rugged individuals, and its citizens still love to live high, wide, and handsome, and have a good time. After all, Texas used to be a nation! Since the days of the Republic of Texas, its citizens have been proud of the state's cowboy traditions. Even the most conservative of its churches love a good party—called "fellowship"—and I grew up with those customs. My Baptist family loved a good "dinner on the grounds and ice cream social" after church—and, yes, I peeked in the door to watch my parents dancing in the living room to swing music after I was supposed to be in bed.

The roots of my interest in the Texas Cowboys' Christmas Ball can be traced to 1982, when my mother gave me a copy of a book by Jim Bob Tinsley entitled *He Was Singin' This Song* (1981). That book, as well as the events at the National Cowboy Poetry Gathering in Elko, Nevada, inspired me to record an album called "Cowboy Songs" in 1989, which quickly became my best-selling album. Tinsley, a University of Florida professor and western-style musician, included in his book Larry Chittenden's poem "The Cowboys' Christmas Ball," which was written about 1889. Tinsley also reproduced the music with its lively-metered lyrics, and mentioned how cowboys sang the six-stanza poem around evening campfires on western ranges. I was fascinated with the way the song described the original Texas Cowboys' Christmas Ball, with humor and colorful language.

Jim Ed Norman, producer of my recordings at Liberty Records (EMI), became the head of Warner Brothers Records-Nashville in the mid-1980s. I followed him to Warner Brothers. Jim Ed wanted an album from me right away, but I knew it would take time to finish the album I was working on at the time, *Tonight We Ride.* To get something out right away, I thought a Christmas song would be perfect, so I recorded my edited version of Chittenden's "The Cowboys' Christmas Ball" with Riders in the Sky in 1985. Jim Ed liked it so much he wanted to save it for a later Christmas album, having recently been successful with Ann Murray's now classic masterpiece Christmas album. But he didn't think the time was right for another Christmas album. So I turned my attention to finishing *Tonight We Ride,* and put "The Cowboys' Christmas Ball" on the shelf.

But I was still fascinated with the Cowboy Christmas song and ideas contained in the images evoked by the song. In 1985, I produced a series of Cowboy Christmas Ball dances in Taos, New Mexico. The events were wildly successful, and I continued the idea in Taos 1986, adding a Cowboy Christmas Ball in Amarillo. But, by 1987, things were different—for a very significant reason.

In 1985 I had been thinking of organizing an event I called "WestFest"—a tribute to the arts, culture, and music of the Old and New West. So . . . in January 1986, at the urging of Willy Matthews, who had designed my first album cover and package, *Geronimo's Cadillac* (and later, many more, including *Cowboy Christmas*), I attended the second Cowboy Poetry Gathering in Elko, Nevada. Willy believed that I should consider cowboy poet Waddie Mitchell as the emcee of my WestFest concept, so I went to Elko—and it was a revelation! Here were men and women of the West I could understand, reciting poems about the West and singing the classic old cowboy tunes and new ones they had composed about cowboy life. I had always tried to be a poet of my beloved West, and now I had met my long-lost artistic family!

The first WestFest, held Labor Day weekend in 1987 at Copper Mountain, Colorado, was a huge success. People loved the mix of Native American dancing, Western art, and cowboy poetry and music with contemporary country music stars. By Christmas I had invited cowboy artists I met in Elko and who had presented at WestFest, to my Cowboy Christmas Ball in Amarillo—such as Don Edwards, Ian Tyson, Chris Ledoux, and Waddie Mitchell. The Taos and Amarillo events grew into today's Cowboy Christmas Tour, which has included many American states and several Canadian provinces.

In late 1989, riding high on the success of several WestFest events in Copper Mountain, I released an album called *Cowboy Songs.* The success of that album led to a request by Jim Ed Norman to produce my Christmas album for Warner Brothers—at last! I reminded him of my recording of "The Cowboys' Christmas Ball" with Riders in the Sky, and we decided to add Suzy Bogguss and Don Edwards to my original recording of the song. In 1991, I released *Cowboy Christmas—Cowboy Songs Vol. II,* featuring Waddie Mitchell as cowboy poet narrator. It was a hit, and this led to more Cowboy Christmas balls and concerts.

In 1992, I received an invitation from the folks in Anson to perform at their Texas Cowboys' Christmas Ball. I was surprised! I didn't know a dance similar to the one described in Chittenden's 100-year-old poem was still going on! I was honored to be asked, accepted the invitation, and in 1993 I appeared in the historic Pioneer Hall in Anson, Texas, accompanied by my Rio Grande Band, featuring Gary Roller, David Coe (his command of old-time fiddle playing was essential), and my son, Ryan Murphey. I was amazed to see so many people in attendance dressed like late nineteenth-century cowboys or old-time cattlemen and their Victorian-dressed spouses (for some it wasn't a costume), mixed with young and older folks in modern western clothes and gear. In my performance, I included classic cowboy songs and instrumental dance tunes of the 1880s, along with my pop and country hits, Bob Wills–style western swing, and contemporary cowboy songs. Although the old-timers were skeptical at first, by the end of the night they approved. They fed us like cattle kings at midnight. Later, those midnight meals led to the release of *The Texas Cowboys' Christmas Ball: Ranch Supper Cookbook.* Like most Texans, I'd always enjoyed a good honky-tonk, I grew to love the idea of a no-smoking, no-drinking, family dance. Today, the event represents a renewed interest in cowboy culture.

The Anson Texas Cowboys' Christmas Ball reflects the historical West

Texas range life and cattle-country rural activities. A winter dance was one of the few times during the year when cowboys of the Old West might get free to attend a "big-time" social event. They dressed up for the occasion. They came early. They stayed late. And they had Texas-sized good times! For single men and women, such a dance provided a time to meet and get acquainted. For married couples with families, it was a romantic moment for generations to celebrate. And if the winter dance was held during the holidays, the meaning of Christmas was not lost in the celebration.

Much about the Texas Cowboys' Christmas Ball remains the same in recent decades, but a few things have changed. Modern technology has improved acoustics. I added large screens on either side of the Pioneer Hall stage, showing photos and film footage of past cowboy ball events, plus scenes of cowboy life. Ball patrons are more diverse in race and ethnicity. Younger people represent a larger percentage of the folks in attendance—and they love the old-time dances!

The best thing that's happened since I started performing at the Anson ball is involvement of the dedicated archivists of Texas Tech University's Southwest Collection in Lubbock. I persuaded a cowboy poet and western musician, Andy Wilkinson, also a Texas Tech teacher, archivist, and historian at the Southwest Collection, to study the Anson Ball. Andy invited archivists Monte Monroe, Curtis Peoples, and Elissa Stroman to Anson. They realized, as I had, that the history and artifacts of the Texas Cowboys' Christmas Ball must be preserved, and through their work with Suanne and Bernie Holtman, other members of the Texas Cowboys' Christmas Ball committee, and friends of the Ball, there is now an archive of this treasured tradition in the Southwest Collection.

Monte Monroe invited historian and writer Paul Carlson, professor emeritus at Texas Tech University, to the Texas Cowboys' Christmas Ball and as a result, Carlson has written an engaging book that recounts its history and evolution. More than a simple narrative, the book places both the original 1880s dances and the modern Texas Cowboys' Christmas Ball within a larger framework. It examines the Anson ball in the broad perspective of similar wintertime dances in late nineteenth-century West Texas. Carlson provides the most thorough biography of Larry Chittenden in print, and analyzes Chittenden's poetry. There is a chapter on cowboy poetry and western dance in general, and the book describes the events, places, and persons mentioned in Chittenden's poem "The Cowboys' Christmas Ball."

Foreword

The American cowboy of the Old West is a national symbol, an icon of popular culture, a common, rural workingman who became a folk hero. Cowboys have become part of an American epic that is commemorated around the globe. Their image is burned deep into our country's collective consciousness, and, annually at cowboy poetry gatherings, cowboy Christmas events, and the Texas Cowboys' Christmas Ball, Americans celebrate the life and culture of western ranch hands, in this case especially cowboys and their contemporaries at play.

Larry Chittenden was a New Yorker who became a cowboy. He bought a large ranch in Jones County northwest of Anson, and he worked both fall and spring roundups with his cowhands. After the spring roundup, he spent the summer on Connecticut's Long Island Sound shore. His most famous poem, written while at home on the ranch in Jones County, was published in 1893 in his first book of poetry, *Ranch Verses.* The book and the poem became widely popular in America and Europe.

Paul Carlson has done a masterful job describing the poem and the dance that inspired it. Whether read by lantern light in a horse camp or in an easy chair, you'll enjoy this adventure into a genuine, nineteenth-century cowboy dance that now boasts an international reputation. In the folksy vernacular of cowpunchers captured by Larry Chittenden as he spoke of Windy Bill Wilkerson, the original dance-caller at the Ball: "Oh, Bill I won't forget yer, and I'll oftimes recall /that lively-gaited sworray—the Cowboys' Christmas Ball."

Michael Martin Murphey
Rocking 3M Ranches: Beulah, CO/ Red River, NM/ Westby, WI/ Bushland, TX

PREFACE

The Texas Cowboys' Christmas Ball is a folk dance festival that carefully re-creates a frontier celebration first held in Anson, Texas, during the mid-1880s. Nearly 130 years later, local and regional leaders continue to stage the event in Anson the weekend before Christmas. It has become an American icon with something of a worldwide reputation. People from Canada, Europe, Australia, and elsewhere have attended the popular folk dance and historical reenactment.

The original dance in Anson is described in William Lawrence "Larry" Chittenden's famous poem, "The Cowboys' Christmas Ball." Printed in the local newspaper in 1890, the rhyming composition became famous after it appeared in Chittenden's book of poetry, *Ranch Verses*, published in 1893. A few years later cowboys and other ranch hands were singing the poem around evening campfires, and the book, highly popular in England and in the American West and South, went through twelve printings in the first dozen years after it was released.

The Texas Cowboys' Christmas Ball is a beautiful reenactment of the 1885 Anson dance. Performed annually since 1934—seventy-nine consecutive years as of this writing—the dance attracts people from great distances. One year people representing thirty-four states were in attendance, enjoying western pioneer music and cowboy dancing reminiscent of 1880s-style frontier celebrations. At the time of this writing in 2013, the ball remained a gala affair, which honors a newly married couple, rekindles a grand party of old, and commemorates one of the nation's first acknowledged cowboy poets and his lively Christmas-dance poem.

No formal history of the modern event or its background and evolution exists. Brief articles are available in journals, magazines, newspapers, and encyclopedias. All are compelling and engaging, but most emphasize recent years, and none makes use of the six large boxes of Texas Cowboys' Christmas Ball Association records at Texas Tech University's Southwest Collection/Special Collections Library.

The present study modestly seeks to provide the missing narrative. In clean, honest prose it attempts to offer a reasoned and documented history of the annual Christmas ball as described in Chittenden's poem and to present a more thorough study than is currently available of the December reenactments.

But its purpose goes beyond a simple explanation of the famous poem and the modern celebration. The book attempts to place the Anson dance in a larger, broader perspective. Accordingly, it examines the evolution of "cowboy," or country music, dances in West Texas and cowboy, or folk, poetry in general; recounts the history of Anson and Jones County; reviews the life and work of Larry Chittenden; and explicates the popular poem. Designed for a wide, general audience, the book looks at the annual Christmas Ball's deep past, investigates its more recent history, and assesses its current status. Maps and photographs illustrate the text.

Many people contributed to this work by providing thoughtful ideas, helpful suggestions, useful information, or other kinds of special assistance. Monte L. Monroe, archivist at Texas Tech University's superb Southwest Collection/Special Collections Library, was with me from the beginning, urging me to undertake the study, offering opinions, and reading and editing the manuscript even as it was being written. He was the driving force behind the study, and, in what turned into a major contribution, he oversaw the selection and collation of most of the photographs.

Likewise, Michael Martin Murphey was important. For several years the Grammy Award–winning artist wanted someone to write a history of the Texas Cowboys' Christmas Ball and, ultimately, he convinced me to take on the project. He provided substance and passion to the study and showed me how the current Texas Cowboys' Christmas Ball fits into a much larger tradition of contemporary cowboy Christmas concerts.

Curtis Peoples, director of the Southwest Collection's Crossroads of Music Archive, and his assistant Elissa Stroman helped in many ways. Among other things, they guided me through the many layers of material in the Texas Cowboys' Christmas Ball Association records, aided with photo collection, and provided important computer searches. In addition, Curtis prepared the maps.

Andy Wilkinson, a multiple Spur Award–winning writer and performance artist, provided suggestions, read and commented on portions of the manuscript, and pointed me to important sources. He helped a lot.

I am indebted to many others, including Robert Weaver, John Perrin, Fredonia Paschal, Connie Aguilar, Diane Warner, H. Allen Anderson, Kindle Parker, John Holmes, and Tai Kriedler at the Southwest Collection. Randy Vance, in the Southwest Collection's reading room, and his student assistants (Nicci Hester, Austin Allison, Sruthi Yadlapti, Rui Su, Maja Milankovic, Emily Henry, and Bojana Ristic) were of enormous help in finding information, completing computer searches, retrieving materials, and negotiating the Collection's archives. David Murrah in Rockport, Cheryl Lewis in Hamlin, Paul Davidson in Levelland, Kimberly Vardeman and Tom Rohrig in the Texas Tech Library, Winston Sosebee in Midland, Alvin Davis in Lubbock, Pat Keen Henley in Plano, Elmer Petersen in Galesburg, Wisconsin, and Scott Sosebee, at Stephen F. Austin State University, provided information.

Becky Davidson and Kay Spears proved wonderfully cooperative. Davidson, a native of Anson and an employee in Texas Tech University's Graduate School, allowed me to borrow heavily from her scholarly and thoughtful article on Larry Chittenden's delightful poem, and with her husband pointed me to unknown sources on the idea of "no dancin' in Anson." Spears, who heads the Anson–Jones Museum in Anson, provided photos, information, and important documents associated with the Texas Cowboys' Christmas Ball.

Also in Anson and Hawley, Suanne Holtman and Bernie Holtman, the heart and soul of the modern Texas Cowboys' Christmas Ball, and John Compere, whose family through many generations has maintained a connection to the event, guided me through places connected to Larry Chittenden's Jones County ranch days. Over coffee in Pioneer Hall, we talked about the dance and its history, and they shared with me information and artifacts associated with Chittenden, Anson, and the modern dance celebration. Compere brought along an Abilene hotel register dating to 1890. The register with Larry Chittenden's signature showed that the poet had stayed at the Palace Hotel before moving to his ranch near Anson. After coffee and much good conversation, we drove around Anson and Jones County, looked through the Chittenden corner in the public library, and worked through deed records in the county courthouse. Hard-working and enthusiastic members of the Texas Cowboys' Christmas Ball Association, the Holtmans and Compere are highly knowledgeable about the annual dance's past and actively engaged in its continuing promotion. They also read through portions of the manuscript, corrected errors, and suggested changes.

John T. "Jack" Becker, associate librarian at the Texas Tech University Library, was particularly helpful. He provided information, facilitated library searches, read the manuscript, and offered suggestions of all kinds, including material to include and writing to polish. I leaned heavily on Jack, whom others have called an "editor from hell."

I acknowledge the anonymous reviewers at Texas Tech University Press. I took their advice to heart, followed most of their suggestions, and the work is a better book because of their comments. I am likewise thankful for the help and encouragement of Judith Keeling, the former editor-in-chief at the Press, and Joanna Conrad, assistant director of the Press. They pushed and pulled the manuscript into a book.

My wife Ellen Carlson was, as usual, patient and understanding even during the long hours I spent with the word processor in my little office at home. I was late to her carefully prepared evening dinners far more often than was reasonable or fair as I tried to find a lost reference, finish an uncooperative paragraph, or double check a footnote. To her and to all the others I am deeply grateful.

Dancin' in Anson

CHAPTER ONE

Texas Cowboys' Christmas Ball: The Background

It started as a wedding dance; it became a national treasure. It started as a local celebration; it became an American icon. This grand event, the Texas Cowboys' Christmas Ball, occurs in the small town of Anson, Jones County, Texas, each December. It is a beautiful, family-oriented pageant and dance that enjoys an international reputation, attracting people from across the United States and from Canada, Europe, and elsewhere. The modern, but frontier-style, gala is a stirring and lively experience that reenacts a special cowboy dance from late nineteenth-century Texas.

A unique event, it is organized and maintained by hard-working members of the Texas Cowboys' Christmas Ball Association, who staunchly and stubbornly insist that the dance adhere to traditions of the cattle trail and Western ranch, including pioneer dress clothes, dance steps, and music of the 1880s cattle frontier. By rigorously re-creating the pioneer dance customs, the Association links our urban, industrial, and modern society to our rural, agricultural, and frontier past. Their educational, festive, and colorful dance brings people of diverse cultural, demographic, and geographic backgrounds together in a spirit of perfect equality and harmony, and in doing so, keep noble, time-honored traditions and a favorite pastime of the Old West alive.[1]

The Texas Cowboys' Christmas Ball takes its inspiration from an Anson dance and a popular poem that describes it. The dance occurred in the mid-1880s, nearly 130 years ago. The poem, entitled "The Cowboys' Christmas Ball" and written by William Lawrence "Larry" Chittenden in 1890, became

Anson in Relation to Southwestern Cities. Map by Curtis Peoples. Courtesy of Curtis Peoples.

famous, especially in the South and West, after it was published in Chittenden's best-selling book of poetry, *Ranch Verses.*

It's an engaging story. It began when Anson hotelier M. G. Rhoads and several local citizens—ranchers, cowhands, and townspeople—determined to have a dance party just before Christmas about 1885. They invited everyone in the farming and ranching country in and around Jones County to attend and made plans for a big event, plans that included celebrating the forthcoming wedding of Sam Morrow, a popular cowboy, and Sara Slaton, the daughter of a local farmer.[2]

Such dance parties were not uncommon. Across much of northern West Texas many large ranches and some smaller ones in the late nineteenth cen-

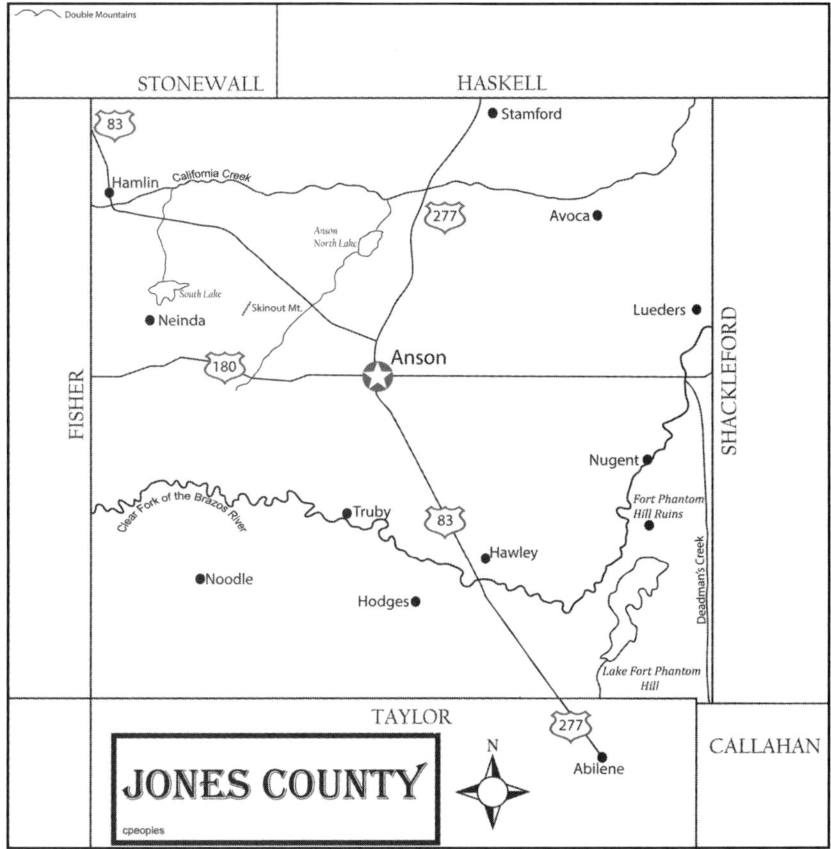

Jones County Features. Map by Curtis Peoples.

tury took turns holding a big party—or "blow out," as they often called it—usually during the winter, at Christmas time or perhaps in January, when ranch activities slackened a bit. New Year's Eve was a popular time for such shindigs, but one could find them held during annual Fourth of July celebrations, at Thanksgiving, or other holidays popular along the frontier.[3]

The winter dances were polite, fancy affairs that might last all night. When one large ranch, the LIT, in the Texas Panhandle held its party, remembered a participant, the ranch manager, "knowing the neatness of cowboys generally," inspected each boy as he walked across the floor in front of him "and unless he could put his feet on the line drawn, he was not permitted to dance that night."[4] Ranch leaders wanted all of their employees who attended the big parties to be sober and well-dressed.

Larry Chittenden, c. 1890s.
Courtesy of Texas Cowboys' Christmas Ball Association.

They usually were. But, if historian William Curry Holden is correct, sometimes "a reckless individual would become rollicky" from too much "ranchman's ball eggnog, [which] was often served . . . and would have to be ejected by his more sober companions." Such an event "was to be expected, and produced no undue commotion."[5]

Married cowhands, townsmen, and ranch managers, as well as resident ranch owners, brought their wives and usually their children with them. From a single cowboy's point of view, older female children and younger single women were especially welcome.

All who attended took care to present themselves in their best attire. Cowboys polished their boots, or even secured new ones. They might buy new clothes from a local merchant or order a special shirt from the catalogue of a distant mail-order company. The few women who could afford one might secure a new dress, but most women cut, stitched, and sewed a new one, or trifled with a dress they already owned to make it festive. Often weeks went into such preliminaries.

The Frying Pan Ranch made elaborate preparations. When the ranch hosted its first "blow out" in the early 1880s, Kate Wetzel, wife of the manager, and William Trescott, the ranch cook, baked, cooked, and prepared for a week for the January event. Warren Wetzel, the Frying Pan manager, ordered oysters from Dodge City, Kansas. Packed in a tin box and covered with ice, the oysters, delivered on the stagecoach, were still frozen when they reached the Frying Pan.

Mrs. Wetzel recalled that guests "came from a distance of eighty miles or more." As people arrived in the afternoon, the Frying Pan hosts offered the arrivals hot coffee, sandwiches, and doughnuts. They served supper about nightfall, and afterward, "we danced all night," with the waltz, schottische, and quadrille (square dance) among the more popular dances. About seventy-five people attended, only twenty of whom were women, but several men, those willing to dance the female part in the quadrilles and perhaps some of the other dances, tied bandanas around their left arm to signify their willingness. At midnight the Wetzels brought out the oysters, a surprising and delightful treat that was one of the highlights of the party. At dawn, Trescott and his helpers prepared breakfast for everyone, after which the Frying Pan cowhands bid their tired guests a safe journey home.[6]

In 1895, the large LS Ranch in Oldham County hosted a dance. This time the Christmas party took place in the ranch bunkhouse. The owners, Charles Whitman and his sister Mrs. Lucien Scott, hired the Kimball String Band from distant Trinidad, Colorado, to provide the music, and the ranch manager, Jordan Edgar McAllister, called out the quadrille dance steps. At midnight, Whitman and his sister provided a large supper in the bunkhouse dining room. The meal included oysters shipped from Denver in ice-packed wooden kegs. They also provided huge amounts of Arbuckle coffee, the favorite such brew in West Texas, and the LS guests danced until dawn.[7]

The first Christmas dance in Anson was not very different. It occurred in 1884 or 1885 in M. G. Rhoads' Star Hotel. Cowhands from area ranches, ranch managers and their wives and children, and townspeople attended. Food, and lots of it, was part of the hotel dance party and most likely with males again outnumbering females, some men, at least during the quadrilles, agreed to dance the female parts. Older, perhaps simplified, versions of modern square dance patterns, such as quadrilles and lancers, were the most popular dances at the Star Hotel that night, but the guests enjoyed waltzes, polkas, reels, and schottisches as well.

Indeed, a typical winter dance program might be similar to one used in neighboring Taylor County in 1886:

1. Grand circle round-up march.
2. Horse hunters' quadrille.
3. Catch-horse waltz.

4. Saddle-up lancers. (Lancers consisted of a set of five quadrilles, each with a different meter.)
5. Broncho racquet. (A racquet was a quadrille variant that included a clogging step.)
6. Captain's quadrille.
7. Circular's galop. (A forerunner of the modern polka, it was a springy step in 2/4 time with a glissade [glide step that usually connects two steps] and chase [sliding step in which one foot "chases" and displaces the other]. Leaders usually introduced a galop after a slow dance.)
8. Round-up lancers.
9. Cut-out schottische.
10. Branding quadrille.
11. Cow and calf racquet.
12. Night-horse lancers.
13. First guard waltz.
14. Second guard quadrille.
15. Third guard Newport.
16. Fourth guard quadrille.
17. Day herders' waltz.
18. Maverick's polka.
19. Bull caves' medley.
20. Stampede all.[8]

The picture above is an original drawing by a Dallas artist, expressing his conception of the Cowboys' Christmas Ball in Anson as described by Larry Chittenden in his ballad some fifty years ago. The ball is to be re-enacted in Anson high school gymnasium Christmas night under auspices of the Parent Teachers' association. The Dallas News gave a streamer Monday on the radio page featuring the Bird-[illegible] and Cowboys in rendition on station WFAA of Chittenden's "Cowboys' Christmas Ball." Attention was called to the fact that the poem constituted a special feature of the National Folk Festival held in Dallas last summer at the Texas Centennial.

Illustration of the Cowboys' Christmas Ball: "That Lively Gaited Sworray." Courtesy of Anson–Jones Museum.

In a March 1903 *Lubbock Avalanche* article, a young woman described her experience at a western ball—although neither the paper nor the woman mentioned the year she attended. Whenever the ball occurred, she had just arrived from the East and as the article suggested, she was unfamiliar with western dancing and admitted to being a bit intimidated. Her first dance was a rollicking quadrille.

She noted: "It was with many misgivings in spite of my partner's assurance that he would pull me through, that I took my place in the dance.

'Hark ye partners.
Rights the same.'

"So far, I bowed as did the rest.

'Balance you all.'

"With the plunge of a maddened steer, my partner came toward me. I smothered a scream as I was seized and swung around like a bag of meal. Before I could get my breath I was pushed out to answer to.

'First lady to the right;
Swing the man that stole the sheep,
Now the one that hauled it home,
Now the one that ate the meat,

Illustration of the Star Hotel, 1885, by Rhea J. Vernon. Courtesy of Anson–Jones Museum.

Now the one that 'gnawed the bones.'

"Not being well acquainted with the private histories of the men in the set, I was at little disadvantage, but I was seized, swung, and passed on to the next, until I finally arrived breathless at the starting point.

'First gent, swing yer opposite pardner,
Then yer turtle dove.
Again yer opposite pardner,
And now yer own true love.'

"I blushed in spite of myself at so publicly passing as my partner's 'turtle dove' and 'own true love,' while his sweetheart over in the corner, transfixing me with a jealous glare, saw no humor whatever in the situation.

"Again came the command:

'First couple to the right,
Cage the bird, three hands round.'

"I found myself in the center of a circle formed by my partner and the second couple and then exchanged places with my partner at the call:

'Birdie hop out and crane hop in,
Three hands around and go it again.
All men left; back to the partner,
And grand right and left.
Come to yer partner once and a half
Yaller hammer right and jaybird left,
Meet yer partner and all chaw hay,
You know where and I don't care,
Seat your partner in the old arm chair.'

"By this time, feeling quite bruised and battered, I was ready for most any kind of a chair."[9]

Clearly, then, in the northwestern cattle country of Texas "cowboy" dance parties were energetic and lively. They were also popular, fairly widespread, and at least on an annual basis common. In Jones County, among the first of such dances occurred at Truby, about seven miles south of Anson on a crossing of the Clear Fork of the Brazos River. The Truby crossing stood on a popular business and trade route between Anson and Abilene, to the south just across the line in Taylor County. At the spot in 1883, county citizens built a wooden bridge across the river, expecting it to ease traffic between the neighboring county seats and increase business. It did. And, upon completion of the bridge in June, local residents in celebration of the finished structure "hung lanterns on the bridge and used it for a dance platform."[10]

When the first dances took place at Anson's Star Hotel, Jones County was small in population: about 546 people in 1880. Most of its inhabitants lived

Leonora Barrett, c. 1954, founder of the modern Texas Cowboys' Christmas Ball. Courtesy of Anson–Jones Museum.

on farms and ranches scattered through the rolling prairie country. Phantom Hill, located southwest of the old site of Fort Phantom Hill in southeastern Jones County, served as the temporary county seat in the summer of 1881 when the county was organized. In November, Jones City became the permanent county seat. At the time, the tiny village with its one dusty street claimed twenty citizens and held four buildings: a store, the residences of Martin Duvall and J. M. Anderson, and a hotel, the Tipton Inn.[11]

Within a year, with Jones City's name changed to Anson, the county seat community had grown. The booming little town contained a small courthouse, seven businesses, two livery stables, a blacksmith shop, thirty residences, a church and school house, and two hotels (the Tipton Inn and the Star Hotel). Also in 1882, William McD. Bowyer, a merchant, established a mail service between Phantom Hill and Anson and shortly afterward he became the community's first federal postmaster.[12]

As indicated, the earliest Anson cowboy Christmas balls were held in the Star Hotel (or, if one prefers, the Morning Star Hotel, as it is called in Jones County histories and in Larry Chittenden's poem, or Lone Star Hotel, as someone who knew most of the participants called it). Built by M. G. Rhoads in 1883, it was located near the square in downtown Anson. Although a small, two-story, wood-frame building, the "posh" hotel, as it has been described, was a popular meeting place in town. Rhoads, hoping

Hybernia Grace, c. 1950s, a social studies teacher at Anson High School was, with Leonora Barrett, instrumental in organizing the reenactments in 1934 and afterward. This photo is c. 1950s. Courtesy of Anson–Jones Museum.

to promote his hotel and increase his business, organized along with some friends, the first Anson Christmas dance in 1884 or 1885. As previously mentioned, the dance also celebrated the January-scheduled wedding of a popular young couple. People came from distant parts of the county, from Abilene, and even from Scurry County. Among those in attendance in 1885, of course, was Larry Chittenden, and after attending a second and perhaps a third Christmas dance in Anson, he wrote his famous poem, first published in the local newspaper in 1890.[13]

To create space for the dance, Rhoads and his wife removed tables and large chairs from the dining room. They lined the walls with smaller chairs, and, because at such dances there was never enough regular seating, writes William Curry Holden, "the deficiency was made up by laying boards across chairs and boxes."[14] While they waited their turn to dance, people at the Star Hotel sat or stood in the parlor, playing whist or dominoes, visiting with one another, drinking coffee, and otherwise trying to be patient. In 1885, Chittenden sat here for several hours observing the dancers and their western folk-dance steps.

Despite such crowded conditions, or perhaps because of them, the dances for unmarried ranch hands and cowboys proved popular. They represented a rare opportunity to meet young, single women for young men in ranch country. In Potter County, for example, Kate Wetzel, one of the first Anglo women in the area, provided occasion for a not untypical experience. Ed Beard, a cowhand from a neighboring ranch, in the early 1880s rode to Wetzel's Frying Pan Ranch on business one afternoon. Beard had not seen a woman in some time. When he saw the young and beautiful Mrs. Wetzel standing in the door of the headquarters building, he was stunned—he could not speak. Wetzel, wrote a biographer, "was wearing a white apron, her hair was auburn and wavy," and Beard later said she "looked so pretty . . . he thought he was having a vision of Heaven."[15]

Ranch life was not easy for cowhands like Ed Beard. Many left the business after only a few years on the range, but some spent their entire adult lives chasing cows, branding calves, and castrating young bulls. The work was harsh, brutal, and unromantic, and, of course, most of it was done on foot rather than in the saddle. Cowboys tended to drive cattle, mainly two-year-old steers, to market, and some of the drives were long, taking the young herders to Kansas, Colorado, Wyoming, or the Dakotas. Older and more experienced cowhands tended to stay near the home ranch. Like Ed Beard, many cattle industry employees were single, and dances were fine places to become acquainted with older girls and younger women.

Thus, when word went out that a ranch, such as the Frying Pan, or a business, such as the Star Hotel, had scheduled a dance, cowhands, ranch managers, townspeople, and others made plans to attend. People who heard or read in a local newspaper about such a winter-time dance considered

Old gymnasium at Anson High School, c. 1930s. Courtesy of Texas Cowboys' Christmas Ball Association.

Dancing inside the Anson High School gymnasium, 1938. Frank Reeves photo collection. Courtesy of Southwest Collection/Special Collections Library, Texas Tech University.

themselves invited. As mentioned, plans were made, boots were polished, and clothes laid out. At the appointed time, usually in December or January, folks in great anticipation and full of good cheer rode on horseback, in horse-drawn wagons, or in buggies to the celebration. For instance, Hattie Mae Scott and her brother Fletcher rode twenty-five miles on horseback from Fort Phantom Hill to the first cowboys' Christmas ball in Anson.

At his Star Hotel, M. G. Rhoads served coffee and sweets as the dance guests arrived. A bit later attendees ate an evening meal, one to which many people brought food that Rhoads and others spread out in smorgasbord or buffet fashion. When the food was cleared, the dancing began and went on for several hours, often until dawn. Musicians with a bass viol (bass fiddle or doghouse bass), a tambourine, and a fiddle or two provided the music. For the quadrilles and the lancers, such dance tunes as "Sallie Goodin," "Turkey in the Straw," and "Arkansas Traveler" were popular at the time and were likely performed at the Anson dances.

The Cowboys' Christmas Ball at the Star Hotel in Anson occurred each December for six or seven years. But about 1890 or 1891—probably 1891—Rhoads' popular wood-frame structure burned to the ground, and Rhoads left the hotel business. He sold the lot on which his hotel had stood to D. A. Wood, who in 1892 used rocks in constructing a building in its place, "the first stone building in the business section of Anson," according to a Jones County history. For weeks Wood's son John A. Wood had hauled the rocks and stones by wagon from near Lueders, a community in northeastern Jones County, and from Skinout Mountain, a long, low mesa about eight miles northwest of Anson and close to Larry Chittenden's ranch house.[16]

After the hotel burned and Rhoads left town, the annual cowboys' Christmas ball in Anson went into hibernation, or dry dock as some might say. Similar dances were still held at ranches in Jones County, of course, and in other parts of Texas cattle country, but the popular Anson affair ended—for a time. In 1922, Leonora Barrett, an Anson folklorist and teacher, along with friends, sponsored a cowboy dance in honor of the centennial of Stephen Austin's first trip to Texas. It was not repeated.[17]

But then, in 1934, after a hiatus of forty-two years, Barrett and other women of Anson, including teacher colleague Hybernia Grace, revived the Cowboys' Christmas Ball. They arranged for a "reenactment," as the group called it, to be held in the gymnasium of the local high school where Barrett taught. Amazingly, the determined little group reestablished the event during one of the worst years of America's economic and financial Great Depression.[18]

Because they were reenacting an historical event, Barrett and the others kept the music and instrumentation similar to 1880s standards. Likewise, people in attendance wore clothes reminiscent of the late nineteenth century. The event was a success. They staged it again—and then again. After holding the reenactment at the high school for a few years, Barrett and other leaders moved it into a new building. In 1938, a local contractor with help from employees of the Works Projects Administration (WPA) had begun building Pioneer Hall just beyond the city limits near the city park grounds, and the dance was moved there in 1940. As of early 2013, the Texas Cowboy's Christmas Ball, as it is now known, had been held in the large building for seventy-three consecutive years.[19]

Pioneer Hall is a large rock and brick, arena-like structure of nondescript architecture. The front of the rectangular building faces east across a good portion of the Anson city park, and the county fairgrounds are next door. On the south side there are six windows. Originally, the only door was in the front, but many years later Christmas ball organizers, led by Bernie Holtman, added a second door on the southwest corner. Inside, the building contains a high, rounded ceiling with huge, exposed beams that add rustic Old World charm and a lodge-like ambience to the dance hall. The hardwood dance floor covers over 8,000 square feet, and benches are present on both long sides of the floor. A stage at the west end provides space for bands and other musicians, while on the north side there is space for bleachers or a step-up balcony where dancers can rest and other folks might watch. The building is tobacco- and alcohol-free.

Also in 1937, to support the "reenactment," Christmas ball organizers established a formal organization: The Texas Cowboys' Christmas Ball Association, Inc. Members of the support group came mainly from Anson and other parts of Jones County. Membership was not restricted geographically, but one had to be invited to become a member. Upon establishing the Association, Leonora Barrett secured a copyright to the reenactment pageant, and over the years the copyright has been redrawn and refiled, but remains in effect, meaning that the Association owns the name "Texas Cowboys' Christmas Ball."[20]

The Association also created a board of directors to provide leadership and guidance. In the 1930s, the board included several members with a president, who was always male; a vice president; a treasurer; and a secretary, who was usually female and often the wife of the president. Later the Association

Pioneer Hall, 2012. Courtesy of Monte L. Monroe.

Crowded dance floor inside Pioneer Hall, c. 1960s. Courtesy of Texas Cowboys' Christmas Ball Association.

created the position of historian to keep records, to maintain the "book" (a scrapbook with various documents), and to administer the historical materials that Barrett had assembled over the years.[21] In 2013, Rhonda Weaver served as historian.

Meanwhile, Chittenden's poem was attracting attention. In 1932, Woodward Maurice "Tex" Ritter, who took a scholar's interest in cowboy lore and ballads, recorded, but apparently did not release, a musical rendering of "The Cowboys' Christmas Ball," and in 1946, shortly after World War II, Gordon Graham, a Colorado cowboy folklorist and musician, recorded and published a version of the song. Graham also performed his interpretation of the song at the Anson dance in 1946, and, for many years thereafter, a soloist at Pioneer Hall sang the ballad just before the ball began.[22]

Nonetheless, in this period the annual ball struggled. Attendance at the dance was mixed, finances a problem, and support from the city haphazard. In early 1933, for example, the Anson city council, dominated by evangelical

Christian groups, had passed a law prohibiting dancing in town. A person could be fined between five and fifteen dollars for dancing in the city, and even senior proms at the high school could not be held.[23]

Sadly, young people in Anson in the 1930s and afterward grew up not being allowed to dance in public. Perhaps also they grew into adulthood with the impression that dancing was evil and wrong. In any case, many of them did not participate in the Texas Cowboys' Christmas Ball and in subsequent years many of them opposed holding the popular Christmas-time dance.[24]

More than half a century later the anti-dance ordinance was still on the books. The Texas Cowboys' Christmas Ball in 1940 obtained an exemption from the law, but for reasons not always clear some discord remains between supporters of the annual dance and citizens who continue to oppose dancing in Anson. As late as 1986, for example, a local resident remarked, "I feel like some dance per se is vulgar." He claimed, "The music and some of the rhythms, especially the modern rhythms, appear to me to be the result of native dances that were intended to lead to sexual activity."[25]

Through all such difficulties, the dance with its reenactment of Larry Chittenden's "The Cowboys' Christmas Ball" has continued. The Association and its board, the latter of which meets three times a year, are largely responsible—they have refused to quit. Led in 2013 by president Davis Weaver, enthusiastic leaders such as Bernie Holtman, Suanne Holtman, and John Compere, among others, Association members plan and direct the event. As December approaches, they start getting Pioneer Hall ready, which includes waxing the floor. In December they clean the place and decorate it with mountain cedar, mistletoe, and other trimmings. Other preparations, such as advertisements, invitations, and security needs, are completed as the dance weekend nears. And then every year on the weekend before Christmas, the dance takes place.

Of course, the Christmas Ball has evolved since its revival in 1934. Until the 1950s, for example, it was a four-day event, but since then, it has been staged over a three-day period. Also, as western dance music has changed, dance patterns have shifted. Waltzes and schottisches remain popular, but quadrilles and lancers are danced less frequently. Such older dances as the varsovienne or varsouviana (Put Your Little Foot) and Virginia reel are still performed. The Cotton-Eyed Joe remains popular at old-time western dances, but the ubiquitous shuffle dance, or Texas two-step, remains the most common one. The music is often modern, reflecting changing dance styles.

The grand march, however, still honors a newly married cowboy and his bride, and, of course, the couple leads it and by doing so gets each year's big dance started. It's exciting.

In the end, the Texas Cowboys' Christmas Ball continues to bring people together. It continues to be held the weekend before Christmas. It continues to provide easy, old-style recreation and energetic entertainment. It continues to reflect the traditions of Jones County's pioneer days when holiday dances constituted the big "blow out" of the winter season. And, according to a Jones County history, from the 1880s to the present, the Ball continues to "hold the limelight as Anson's chief link with the more glamorous period of the old time rancher and his working cow-hands."[26]

CHAPTER TWO

Anson and Jones County in the 1880s

When Larry Chittenden's "The Cowboys' Christmas Ball" was written in the late 1880s, Anson was the quiet, little administrative seat of Jones County. In 1880, the town, named Jones City at the time, had a population of twenty, which increased rapidly after Jones City became the county seat in late 1881. By the end of 1882, and with its name changed to Anson, the community had increased to 640 or more. Population growth then relaxed during the next couple of decades, slowed by declining cattle prices, severe drought, and a series of fires that repeatedly consumed much of downtown Anson. Still, in 1910 Anson totaled 1,842 inhabitants, and twenty years later—about the time the big dance party resumed—2,093 people called the city home.[1]

The story of Jones County mirrors that of Anson. Created in 1858 by the Texas state legislature from Bexar and Bosque counties, it was named for Anson Jones, the last president of the Republic of Texas. For two decades the county was home to only a few people. For electoral and other governance purposes, state officials in 1874 attached it to neighboring Shackelford County, and as its population increased it became Precinct No. 5 of that county. Finally, in 1881, some twenty-three years after Jones County was created, residents petitioned for organization. At the time, about 546 people in 154 households lived in the county.[2]

In 1885, when Chittenden attended his first "cowboy" dance in Anson, both the town and the county were prosperous because of the booming western cattle industry. Then changes came. Falling livestock prices, drought, harsh winter storms, barbed wire fencing, and an increasing presence of farmers contributed, however slowly, to a shift in Jones County from open-range livestock operations to fence-enclosed cattle ranching, and ultimately to stock farming. This agricultural evolution throughout the 1880s and 1890s was not unique to Jones County, of course, as it occurred over much of the northern parts of West Texas.

In Jones County, the story began about 1873. John, Creed, and Emmett Roberts and J. G. and Mode Johnson pushed some cattle into grassy lowlands drained by streams emptying into the Clear Fork of the Brazos River in southeastern Jones County. They were among the first permanent settlers. According to local historians Hooper Shelton and Homer Hutto, the Roberts brothers established a camp along "the Clear Fork near the present site of Nugent" about four miles north of abandoned Fort Phantom Hill. About five miles away to the northeast the Johnsons set up headquarters on Chimney Creek. It was "ideal cow country," writes Emmett Roberts. The "grass was abundant; the country was not overstocked . . . ; the winters were mild and [with trees and shrubs along stream banks] the country offered good protection."[3]

Not all was easy. The first ranchers lived in tents, lost horses to Comanche and Kiowa warriors, and worried about losing cattle to mountain lions, wolves, and coyotes. Wolves proved the most troublesome predators, and were especially hard on young animals. Bison (American buffalo) were still present in Jones County in the 1870s, and, while they were not predators, they competed with livestock for grazing land. They might quickly consume all the grass in a particular area before moving on, leaving behind a depleted feeding ground. Moreover, they "cut deep trails [that horses] found too narrow to follow conveniently."[4]

The presence of bison attracted Indian hunters. From their reservation in Indian Territory (Oklahoma), Comanches and Kiowas in the early 1870s rode south across the Red River to hunt. In doing so, they sometimes came across Anglo horse herds in Jones County and raided them. According to Roberts, they seldom stole cattle. To prevent horse thefts, the Roberts brothers "always left camp before daylight and waited until after dark to return," and they moved their camp as soon as "trails" to their camp began to show. Still, horses continued to disappear. Sometimes domestic horses stolen by Native warriors and later released joined wild horses, which were common in Jones County until 1880. The feral animals, noted Roberts, "within a short time [became] as wild as [the] wildest mustang."[5]

Native American raids on area horse herds stopped in the mid-1870s, at about the same time that bison also disappeared from Jones County ranges. The reasons were numerous, including pressure from Native American hunters off their reservations and domesticated livestock. Bison, horses, and cattle competed for the same food sources and, as a result, the appearance of European-based livestock altered bison grazing patterns. Bison, for example, instinctively grazed the most abundant areas. After grazing they moved to another area of relative abundance, not returning to the grazed-over area until it again became the most abundant range. But in competition with horses and other domesticated livestock, such grazing habits began to unravel. In addition, European animals harbored diseases, such as anthrax, brucellosis, and tuberculosis, that negatively affected bison numbers.

Then, in the 1870s bison hide hunters arrived. The tough and unkempt but efficient killers destroyed the last of the large, magnificent beasts. Many Anglo hide hunters saw their work as advancing civilization. "Buffalo hunting," said J. Wright Mooar, "was a business and not a sport; it required capital, management and work, lots of hard work, more work than anything else." Mooar, a most successful hide hunter, said, "the killing of the buffalo [was not] accomplished by vandals." It was an industrial enterprise, he suggested, made possible by better rifles and new hide-tanning technology, and success went to the most skilled and daring of the hunter-businessmen.[6]

From bases first at Fort Griffin in Shackelford County and later at short-lived Rath City in southern Stonewall County, the hide men spread across the rolling plains of West Texas. They systematically slaughtered the ever-decreasing bison herds. In 1877, a small group of surveyors heading for the Llano Estacado crossed through Archer County. One of the men, O. W. Williams, later reported that we ran "through a country marked by a great number of glistening skeletons of buffaloes, apparently slaughtered one or two years earlier." The bleached bones covered two "spots of ten acres each," wrote Williams, with an estimated one hundred "skeletons closely lying, as the result of a hunter getting what was called a 'stand.' "[7]

In Jones County, bison had a similar fate. Emmett Roberts remembered that in about 1873 he "could step out from [his] house or tent and shoot several [bison] early in the morning without moving from in front of the door." Six years later T. J. "Cottonwood" Scott, a farmer-stockman, reportedly killed the last of the big herbivores in the southern Clear Fork River country, and, thus, in 1879 the last bison to graze in Jones County was gone.[8]

As bison disappeared, cattle and livestock men came to dominate the

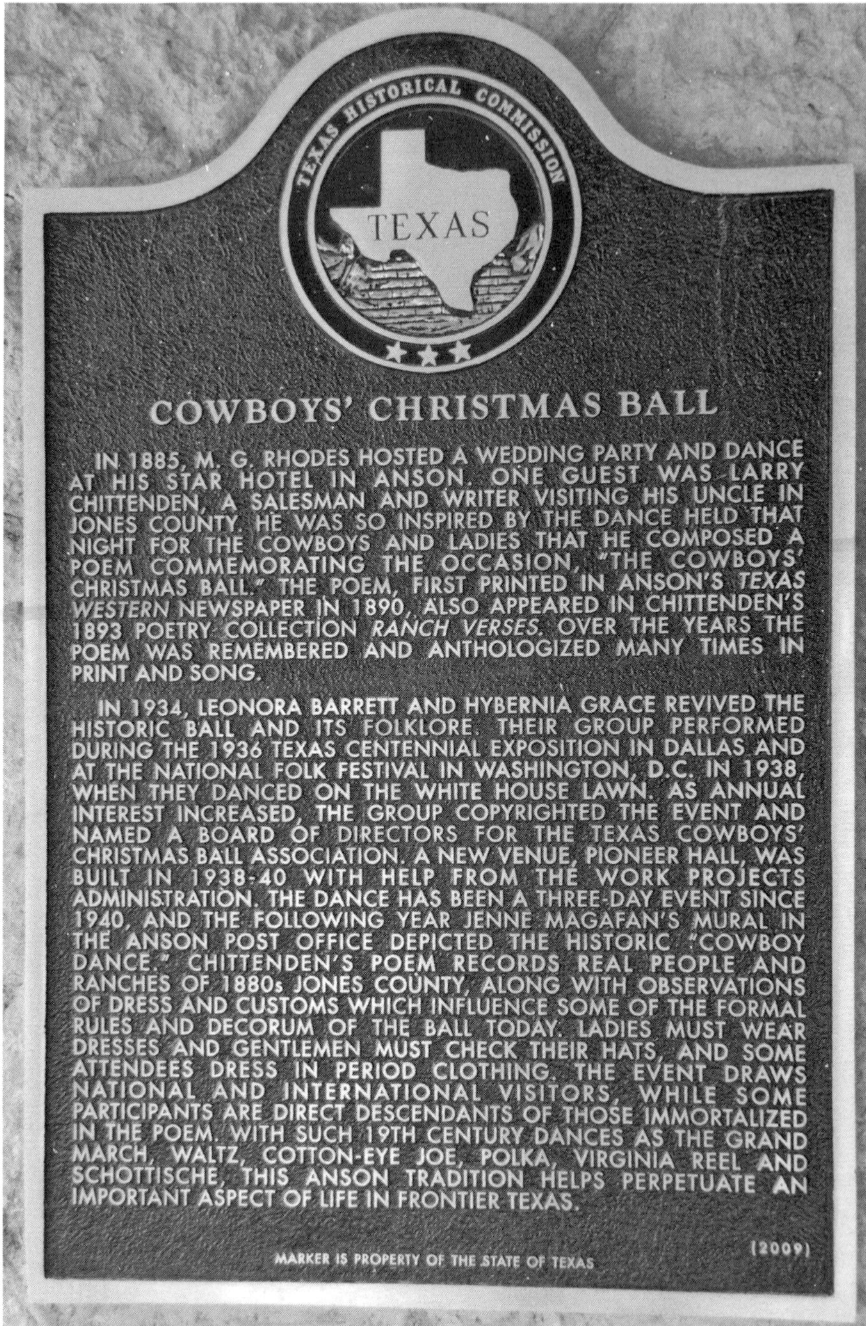

Anson, Texas Historical Commission marker on Pioneer Hall. Courtesy of Monte L. Monroe.

economic life of the county. After the Roberts brothers and the Johnsons arrived in 1873, cowboys drove hundreds of cattle from the eastern areas onto the ranges of Jones County. Their bosses acquired school land—alternate sections (640 acres) in a checkerboard fashion reserved by the state to support education—and purchased railroad land, or as free grazers without land titles they pushed their livestock into unsecured and perhaps unclaimed sections. Emmett Roberts, for example, remembered that we "didn't think the country would ever be settled. Why should we file on land when we had the free use of it anyway?"[9]

Men and women established ranches both large and small through major parts of the county. By the end of the decade cattle outfits included the Roberts Ranch, the Johnson Ranch, the John Merchant Ranch, and several others known by their brands: Pitch Fork, Cross P, T-Diamond, Circle Bar, Horseshoe, and A 7, among others.[10]

One of the other ranches was that of Swante Magnus Swenson, an 1838 Swedish immigrant who divided his time between Austin and New York City. Swenson held railroad certificates dating to 1854 to 100,000 acres of land, part of which was in Jones County. In the late 1870s he began to consider developing the property by raising cattle and convinced his sons Eric Pierson and Swen Alvin to manage the cattle operation—even if from a distance. Swenson and his sons toured the Throckmorton County property and decided to expand their range. They bought alternating sections of school and railroad land until they held some 560 sections in Jones, Throckmorton, Shackelford, Haskell, and Stonewall counties. In 1882 the brothers, using barbed wire, set out to fence their property. They began with fifty thousand acres spread across eastern Jones and western Shackelford counties near modern Lueders. They named it the Ericsdale Ranch, and stocked it with two thousand cattle.[11]

Even as ranching expanded in Jones County, farming got a foothold. "Nesters," as cattlemen called the farmers, began arriving in the late 1870s. During one week in August 1879, for example, farmers driving some forty-seven wagons passed through Fort Griffin on their way to Jones, Taylor, and neighboring counties. The rush to settle up the country was on, and when the Texas and Pacific Railroad reached through northern Taylor County the next year, what had been a stream of westward moving farmers became a flood.[12]

Henry Foster, who had arrived from Missouri in July 1879, may have been the first of the farmer-settlers to till the soil. Quickly, he filed on a homestead in eastern Jones County, built a house, plowed some ground, and planted his first crop—millet. Because of his chance generosity—a meal—to cattlemen Emmett Roberts and Bill Moore, who were riding past his homestead, Foster did not experience any difficulty with livestock men. A few years later Foster opened a small business in Anson. He was "Big Boston" of Chittenden's Christmas ball poem.[13]

Eventually, farmer-settlers planted various crops. But, as Hooper Shelton and Homer Hutto wrote, cotton "developed very early as the most promising 'money' crop." As early as the fall of 1880, a Jones County cotton grower near Mulberry Creek sold a bale of the white fiber in Abilene, which had just been established along the Texas and Pacific Railroad tracks in Taylor County. About 1882, Abe and Sam R. Cox grew three acres of cotton in the Round Mound area, but rather than pick it, they sold the crop as it stood in the field. The buyer, Ernest Zipp, who had arrived in the county in 1879, picked a bale from the plot and hauled it fifty "miles to a gin at Cottonwood Springs in Callahan County."[14]

For reasons not always clear, although Henry Foster's generosity must have had something to do with it, trouble in Jones County between farmers and cattlemen was minimal. Some cattlemen did indeed try to convince T. J. "Cottonwood" Scott that the county was not suited to farming, but he remained unconvinced. Perhaps an important reason for the general lack of mutual mistrust, fence cutting, or even bloodshed—all of which occurred in some Texas counties—was that several Jones County pioneers were farmer-stockmen, settlers who raised some cattle and horses and planted their crops. Some of the early farmer-stockmen included August Lieb, E. M. Douthit, W. J. Herrington, C. A. Fomby, B. E. Louder, S. O. Larche, and A. D. Marcup.

By 1880, Jones County, according to federal census reports, had attracted about 546 people who lived in 154 households. The citizens included cattlemen, cowboys, farmers, farmer-stockmen, and their families. In addition, businessmen and entrepreneurs, seeing opportunities in providing needed services to such early settlers, had arrived. The county was becoming a busy place but most of its population lived along its southeastern edge, especially in the vicinity of long-abandoned Fort Phantom Hill, whose crumbling ruins were still a reminder of West Texas's long martial past.

Then in 1881, local political leaders moved to organize their rapidly growing county. They circulated a petition for organization, collected 185

Anson post office mural depiction of Cowboys' Christmas Ball in early days. Courtesy of Monte L. Monroe.

signatures, and in April presented it to the Shackelford County Commissioners' Court. When the court, which held political jurisdiction over Jones and a few other counties, accepted the request for separation, Jones County leaders moved quickly. They divided their county into four precincts, made Phantom Hill the temporary county seat, and ordered elections to be held for county officers and for the location of a permanent seat of government. Less than two months later the elections occurred, and on June 13 the first commissioners' court met at Phantom Hill. The new court included E. M. Johnston, county judge; W. H. Smith, county clerk; and four commissioners —T. J. Scott, C. J. Chapman, A. Calham, and J. J. Elliott.[15]

The selection of a permanent county seat was more difficult. It took three elections. Jones City (Anson), although a tiny village, received a majority of votes—perhaps because it was located near the county's center. Representatives of Phantom Hill, the county's largest community, objected to the outcome, stating it was illegal because people who had not lived in the county for six months had supported Jones City, forcing a second and then a third vote. Jones City won each of the elections, and on November 14, 1881, the county commissioners declared the then-growing town the permanent seat. Early the next year, Jones City became Anson.[16]

In the 1880s, as the initial Star Hotel Christmas-time dances occurred,

Jones County underwent significant changes. Its population increased more than seven-fold, from about 546 people in 1880 to 3,797 ten years later. The number of cattle on its scattered range lands increased from a few thousand head in 1880 to 20,779 in 1890, with Swenson's SMS ranching empire near modern Stamford responsible for much of the increased numbers of livestock. The amount of land under cultivation increased from 1,191 acres in 1880 to 60,120 a decade later, with farmers producing cotton, wheat, corn, and oats. Anson and Phantom Hill were the largest towns in 1880, but small trade centers and tiny crossroads communities existed at scattered points through the county. In addition, others such as Hawley, Noodle, Truby, and Neinda, appeared during the decade. The present largest town in Jones County, Stamford, was not founded until the turn of the century.[17]

In the 1880s, Anson dominated the economic life of Jones County. As the administrative and judicial center of the county, it quickly attracted businessmen, attorneys, educators, preachers, physicians, and others. Founded where rancher John Merchant had erected a mesquite corral, Anson in 1880 claimed four buildings: William McD. Bowyer's general merchandise store; P. S. Tipton's hotel; and the residences of Martin Duval, the county surveyor, and J. M. Anderson. They were small wood structures, as was the first courthouse, a modest twenty-four by thirty-two-foot box and strip building, which was constructed of lumber that Frank Huie, one of the earliest citizens of Anson, hauled from Abilene in an ox-drawn wagon.

By the end of 1882 Anson had grown. Along its dusty streets, it counted seven business houses, two hotels (the Tipton Inn and the Star Hotel), two livery stables, a blacksmith shop, thirty residences, and a church and school house. Because transportation was a problem, some of the first Anson settlers built their homes from local shinnery and blackjack logs with cracks stuffed with clay mortar. Some people lived in makeshift dugouts or temporarily in tents.[18]

Still, Anson grew. William McD. Bowyer became the first federal postmaster, and before a stagecoach line became established, a hack carried mail and passengers back and forth to Abilene, but, as noted, some mail came by horseback from Phantom Hill. In 1883, Dick Davis established the *Texas Western*, the town's first newspaper. In 1884, the citizens of Jones County at a cost of $2,250 established a new courthouse, a two-story structure that originally had been a hotel. Two years later at a cost of $23,000 they erected a third courthouse in the center of Anson's square, a large brick and stone structure, and sold the second official county building. It became the Maxwell Hotel. The town's population was increasing, although still numbering less than one thousand in 1886, and its business section had become a busy place, attracting cowboys, tradesmen, farmers, travelers, visitors, and others.[19]

By this time, the first of the annual cowboy dances had been held at M. G. Rhoads' Star Hotel. First staged in 1884 or 1885, the dance, which attracted people from around Jones and neighboring counties, had two purposes: to promote the hotel and to honor a young cowboy and his future bride. Rhoads and his wife hired Clarence and Walter Wright of Roby in Fisher County to play fiddles at the dances and for at least one of them they arranged for a bass viol player to come from Abilene. Someone also played a tambourine, but, as Chittenden's poem is an amalgamation of incidents from two or three dances, the four musicians may not have been present at each of the 1880s Christmas-time dances. Indeed, no extant records show whether all four musicians attended each of the popular events.

Larry Chittenden, a newspaperman turned rancher and poet, attended the 1885 dance—and subsequently two or three others. His wealthy uncle, Simeon B. Chittenden, had invested in ranch land near Skinout Mountain, the long, low mesa about seven or eight miles northwest of Anson, and Chittenden was in Jones County to examine the property.

In the late 1880s and early 1890s, while Chittenden developed the ranch property and wrote poetry, changes came to Anson and Jones County. Drought proved the major cause, but harsh winter weather was also a factor. The unusually cold winter of 1885–1886 was hard on livestock, especially cattle as they struggled to forage on the open plains. Then in a long, hard drought, which began in the late spring of 1886, cattle grazed down the over-stocked ranges and constantly decreasing grass resources. On the heels of the dry summer, the poor conditioned cattle had to face another harsh winter in 1886–1887, of extreme cold and unusually high amounts of snowfall. Cattle withered and died. By spring 1887, many western cattle growers, including those in Jones County, were broke and their livestock in very poor shape. The drought persisted into the 1890s, prolonging the financial havoc for ranchers and the stark, physical distress on animals.

As a result, immigration to Jones County slowed and livestock and agricultural production declined a bit. Many people gave up their land and any claims they had filed on it and left the county. For such farmers and farmer-stockmen, optimism turned to gloom as they abandoned their land claims, forfeiting some 22,570 acres. Livestock numbers also declined briefly.[20]

Not everyone gave up, but many families suffered. By the early 1890s, for food some folks turned to jackrabbits, cottontails, and even prairie dogs, which numbered in the thousands in the county. Livestock men sent large numbers of cattle to market. Those few who could afford it fenced their ranges to prevent their loosely herded animals from drifting south with the winter storms. The Swenson Land and Livestock Company fenced each of its three big ranches—Eleonora, Ericsdale, and Mount Albin—in Throckmorton, Jones, Haskell, Shackelford, and Stonewall counties.[21] Likewise, large cattle operations, such as the Pitchfork and Four Sixes (6666), in neighboring counties and ranches in the Texas Panhandle fenced their ranges after the two cold winters sandwiched around the 1886 drought had caused their cattle to drift southward far from their home range. In places where the winters were less difficult, such as in southern Jones County, the severe lack of rainfall caused hardships as well, for cattle drifted down streams seeking water.

In Anson, fires changed the town as well. The Star Hotel burned in 1890 or 1891. Two years later, according to Shelton and Hutto, sixteen of Anson's twenty businesses burned, and about 1896 a fire damaged the Maxwell Hotel, which had been established a decade earlier in the second courthouse building. Mrs. Lois Cowan, daughter of John A. Wood, watched while men using "bucket brigades" attempted to douse the hotel fire but "flames spread to [a] nearby hardware store." The three fires in the 1890s slowed Anson's growth temporarily but also they encouraged citizens to use rock, stone, and brick for building material.[22]

Both Anson and Jones County recovered from the calamities. In Anson after the devastating fire in 1893, people rebuilt the downtown area and repaired or replaced their damaged homes. As noted, rock, stone, and later brick became important new building materials. The city's population increased to just over one thousand people in 1900 and to 1,842 ten years later. In the 1880s and 1890s, Anson was the largest and busiest urban community in Jones County.

Moreover, improved roads connected Anson to smaller villages, hamlets, and crossroads communities throughout Jones County, thus enhancing its position as the county's economic center. Sometimes "improved" roads "meant little more than cutting down trees . . . and finding the best places at

Anson at night, showing the Anson Opera House, the large building to the right, c. 1920s. Courtesy of Anson–Jones Museum.

which streams could be forded." Moreover, many of the first roads were little more than old mail-delivery lines. Still, they marked travel routes. One of them "crossed the southeast corner [of the county] following the old route" of the Butterfield Overland Mail service. In the southwestern part of the county, a mail line connected Phantom Hill to present Snyder in Scurry County. The road from Anson to Abilene was only a trace at first, but after local officials built a bridge across the Clear Fork branch of the Brazos River near Truby in 1883, it became the most frequently traveled road in Jones County.[23]

Anson, along with every community in West Texas, sought rail service. Indeed, lack of a railroad in the 1880s could doom a town, as happened to Fort Griffin when the new railway went to Albany or to Buffalo Gap when the rails went through Abilene. Some towns, such as Belle Plaine in Callahan County, just disappeared. In Belle Plaine's case, the Texas and Pacific Railroad in 1880 passed through Baird eight miles north on its way to Abilene and points west.

In the 1880s, neither Anson nor Jones County got a railroad. But Anson

Bob Weatherby, who danced at the ball in Anson in 1885, and also in 1934 (current photo), and 1955. Frank Reeves photo collection. Courtesy of Southwest Collection/Special Collections Library, Texas Tech University.

persevered and even thrived. It prospered because it was a well-established county seat, conveniently situated in the center of the county, and general proximity and a good road to Abilene, a major rail center in the mid-1880s. Farmers sold most of their feed crops locally in the drought years of the late 1880s, and some who raised cotton hauled it about twenty miles to Albany. If they lived in southern Jones County they hauled it about twenty miles to Abilene.

Anson did not remain Jones County's largest community for long. After the turn of the century, such budding rivals as Stamford in the northeast (established in 1900) and Hamlin in the northwest (established in 1905) appeared. Both communities, having received multiple railroad connections, soon surpassed Anson in population and business activity—in Hamlin's case only for a time.[24] Yet, Anson's success could not be denied, and eventually a railroad, The Abilene and Northern Railway, was built through town connecting Anson with Stamford and Abilene.

Like Anson, Jones County did recover from the drought and the general sluggish economy of the mid-1880s. The recovery was neither easy nor quick. During the dry spell farmers, ranchers, and townspeople all sought to keep up their courage by putting off improvements, by catching fish in the dwindling streams and holding neighborhood fish fries, or by reducing household expenses. All the while, of course, they patiently waited for the return of rain.

When at last precipitation levels improved, Jones County citizens and West Texans in general moved carefully. Many ranchers dug wells, erected windmills, and built dams to hold water. Jones County farmers and cattlemen paid closer attention to managing grass resources, grew more feed crops, upgraded their livestock, and hired cautiously.

Many ranchers made an effort to improve livestock bloodlines. The Swenson syndicate, for example, introduced 125 pure-blood Hereford and Shorthorn heifers on their Ellerslie Ranch north of Anson and southwest of modern Stamford. Their idea was to replace the long-legged, long-backed, and long-tailed longhorns that they had initially brought into the region. Larry Chittenden, living on his uncle's ranch northwest of Anson, was among the first livestock raisers to bring in polled, black Aberdeen Angus cattle to the county, and he quickly added Hereford purebreds.[25]

Farmers likewise paid closer attention to their field crops. Unlike ranchers who could walk their "crop" to market, farmers without railroads close at hand needed to produce feed grains and other products that could be sold locally. Plus they turned to crops that could survive with less water, such as cotton, wheat, and grain sorghum.

The county revived. After the 1886 drought, some folks who had left returned, new homestead filings were settled up, and Anson and several other communities increased in population. Schools appeared everywhere, for education was always important in Jones County, and schools attracted more people. Then at the turn of the century, railroads, some of them short-lived affairs, pushed into the county. The Swenson ranching syndicate was at least partially responsible for some of the railroads, such as the Texas and Central Railroad and the Stamford and Northwestern Railway Company, but entrepreneurs of all kinds invested in railroads in West Texas.

The first railway in Jones County was the Texas and Central. In 1900, Texas Central managers and the Swenson family established Stamford at the end of the proposed line, and the town soon prospered, attracting businessmen, professionals, and others. As owners extended the rail line westward and southward toward Anson, Stamford grew and by the 1920s it had become, as noted above, the largest community in Jones County. In 2013, with a population of 3,124 people, it continued as the county's major urban center.

Railroads, of course, made shipping farm products, such as cotton, easier and cheaper, and partly as a result, cotton became an important farm crop for growers located near a rail line. In the far northwest, rail service also became a major factor in the establishment of Hamlin. Entrepreneurs and town builders planned several railroads through the town and built a couple of them. Eventually, the Atchison, Topeka and Santa Fe passed through the town, and Hamlin responded with an increasing population. In 2013, Hamlin, an important trade center near the Fisher County line, counted 2,124 citizens.[26]

As railroads at last entered Jones County at the turn of the century, Larry Chittenden still tended to his uncle's ranch—at least in the winter. The property northwest of Anson covered nearly ten thousand acres in 1900 and, as indicated, he had upgraded his cattle herd. He owned a lot of horses and mules, about two hundred head by some accounts, and he cultivated two hundred acres of the ranch's best prairie land. Chittenden accompanied his cowboys, riding, hunting, and participating in roundups. He also, as one newspaper reported, spent his time on the ranch "writing verses in his comfortable ranch house."[27] Another favorite place for composing cowboy poetry was the Skinout Mountain mesa, where with a pipe, a pen, and a notebook, he often sat quietly watching the sunset, with the Double Mountains off to the northwest, listening to birds sing.

Each year, soon after the spring roundup Chittenden left Jones County. He headed east to divide his time among several resorts in the vicinity of New York, a place where several members of his extended family lived. One of his favorite destinations was Granite Bay in the Short Beach section of Branford, Connecticut, along the shore of Long Island Sound. He owned or rented a cottage in Short Beach.

Near there stood the "delightful summer home of Ella Wheeler Wilcox." A popular American writer and poet, Wilcox and her husband Robert were "intimate friends" of Chittenden.[28] The Wilcox family had built a few cottages along Long Island Sound at Short Beach, and called the collection of buildings "Bungalow Court," a place where they hosted gatherings with literary and artistic friends. Ella Wheeler Wilcox wrote a large number of poems, one of which, "Solitude," was published in 1883 in *The New York Sun.* It contained the two now-famous lines: "Laugh and the world laughs with you; Weep and you weep alone."[29]

Whether absent or not from the West Texas ranch, Larry Chittenden saw Jones County change. During the years he spent the winter there, the county had evolved from a territory nearly empty of cattle-raising operations and farming homesteads to a settled region marked by busy railroad towns, trade centers, and other manifestations of early twentieth-century civilization. Farms and ranches filled the rolling plains country. Anson, the largest and busiest community at the time, grew and prospered with the county.

Granted, not all was easy for pioneer folks trying to carve out a living along the plains frontier. Periodic but reoccurring drought and harsh weather, but especially drought in the late 1880s and afterward, sometimes retarded economic progress—not only across most of West Texas but also over much of the Great Plains. Some settlers left; they sold out or abandoned their property. Like William Lawrence "Larry" Chittenden, most transcended the hard times and by doing so helped to build Jones County.

Larry Chittenden: His Life and Letters

William Lawrence "Larry" Chittenden (1862–1934) was a dry goods merchant, newspaperman, rancher, poet, intellectual, and adventurer who could not long remain in one place. He moved about the United States from New York to Texas and back to the Atlantic Coast. He spent a few winter seasons on the Bermuda Islands, kept a summer home in Maine, and visited for extended periods of time other places such as Branford, Connecticut, on the shore of Long Island Sound south of New Haven, and Guilford, Connecticut, the ancestral family home located just east of Branford. While in Texas in the 1880s and afterward, he became acquainted with the custom of ranchers and other rural citizens holding large dance parties, and about 1885 he attended one in Anson, Texas, at the community's Star Hotel.

A few years later, about 1890, he wrote the now famous poem "The Cowboys' Christmas Ball." The popular little ballad re-creates the 1885 dance, or perhaps more correctly it is a colorful, rhyming composition in verse that combines descriptions of a series of the annual Jones County wintertime dances. The poem first appeared in Hec McEachern's Anson newspaper, the *Texas Western*, on June 19, 1890, and was published in both the *Galveston Daily News* and the *Dallas Morning News* at the end of December 1891.[1]

Larry Chittenden was born March 23, 1862, at Montclair, New Jersey, the youngest of eight children, to Henry A. and Henrietta Gano Chittenden. The Chittendens were direct descendants of William Chittenden who had come from Cranbrook, Kent, near London, England, in 1639. A participant in the Great Migration of Puritans in the 1630s, when some ten thousand English emigrants moved to New England, William Chittenden settled in Guilford, Connecticut. Nearly three hundred years later, the land and estate, "Mapleside," remained in the Chittenden family, but some of its members had moved to Vermont, New York, New Jersey, or elsewhere.[2]

Larry's father, Henry, became a prosperous New York City clothing and dry goods merchant. With his brother Simeon B. Chittenden, a former New York State legislator, Henry established S. B. Chittenden and Company in Brooklyn. A man of "old time religious zeal," he became one of the founders of Plymouth Church (or Church of the Pilgrims) in Brooklyn and on occasion preached fiery sermons. According to Anson schoolteacher Hybernia Grace, once "when he was still a young unmarried man and in Cincinnati on business for his company, he held one of his impromptu services." His future father-in-law Major Daniel Gano was in the audience that day, heard Henry's lively sermon, and invited the young New Yorker into his home. "Here Henry A. Chittenden met [Major] Gano's daughter" Henrietta.[3]

Larry Chittenden's mother, Henrietta Gano Chittenden, was the daughter of Daniel Gano and Rebecca Hunt Lawrence. Several Gano family members were of French Huguenot descent, and, like many French Huguenots trying to escape an anti-Protestant crusade, fled France in 1689, and settled in New Rochelle, New York. Some members, led by Daniel's preacher-grandfather John Gano, moved into the upper Ohio River Country, with a few like John settling in central Kentucky and others establishing homes in the Cincinnati, Ohio, region. The Ganos became prominent political leaders in Cincinnati and across the river in north-central Kentucky.

Rebecca Hunt Lawrence, Larry Chittenden's maternal grandmother was also a member of a French Huguenot family. Rebecca's ancestors, like the Ganos, had settled in New Rochelle, but later some of them, led by Benjamin Lawrence, moved to Montclair Township, Essex County, New Jersey. Rebecca, as noted, met Major Daniel Gano, in Cincinnati, near where he owned at least three livestock—mainly horses—farms, was the clerk of courts, and operated a large horse-racing track.[4]

After their marriage, Henry A. and Henrietta Gano Chittenden settled in Montclair Township, Henrietta's ancestral family home. Located about twelve miles west of the Hudson River and a few miles northwest of Newark, the township was farming country just before the Civil War. In 1856, the Newark and Bloomfield Railroad Company provided regular service to the area, thus easing any trip to and from Newark or New York City. Soon

Larry Chittenden with dogs on his Jones County ranch in the 1880s or early 1890s. Courtesy of Texas Cowboys' Christmas Ball Association.

a little community that would become the village of Montclair in 1860 was attracting people from both of the neighboring large cities, some seeking a rural residence, some enjoying a Sunday excursion, and some planning a vacation. Montclair, set hard against First Mountain in the Watchung Mountain range, offered a country setting with panoramic views, and its several streams flowing eastward through the township provided wonderful home sites and vacation retreats. Larry Chittenden, in a poem in *Ranch Verses* dedicated to his maternal grandfather Major Daniel Gano, called Montclair "a lovely mountain town."[5]

Larry Chittenden was educated in Montclair and New York City. He loved books, read a lot, and in Montclair as a youth spent a lot of time walking along the banks of neighborhood streams and the hills of First Mountain. Shy and sensitive, he enjoyed the solitude and freedom the mountain brooks of Montclair gave him. Each of his five siblings who survived childhood displayed literary talent, but, according to Hybernia Grace, "Larry is the only one whose poetic instinct was not crushed out by his father."[6]

When Chittenden was born in 1862, the Civil War was underway. His

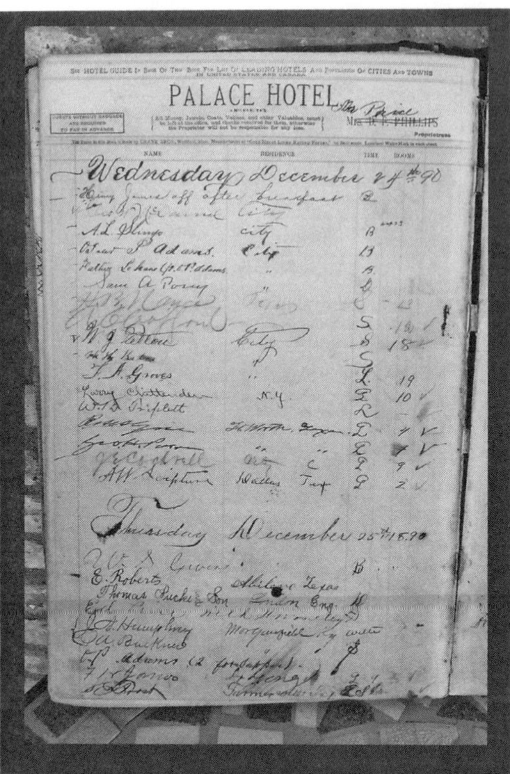

PALACE HOTEL

NAME | RESIDENCE | TIME | ROOMS

Wednesday December 24th 90

A. L. Slimp — city

Larry Chittenden — N.Y. — 10

W. T. D. Triplett

Ft. Worth, Texas

A W Scipture — Dallas Tex — 2

Thursday December 25th 1890

E. Roberts — Abilene Texas

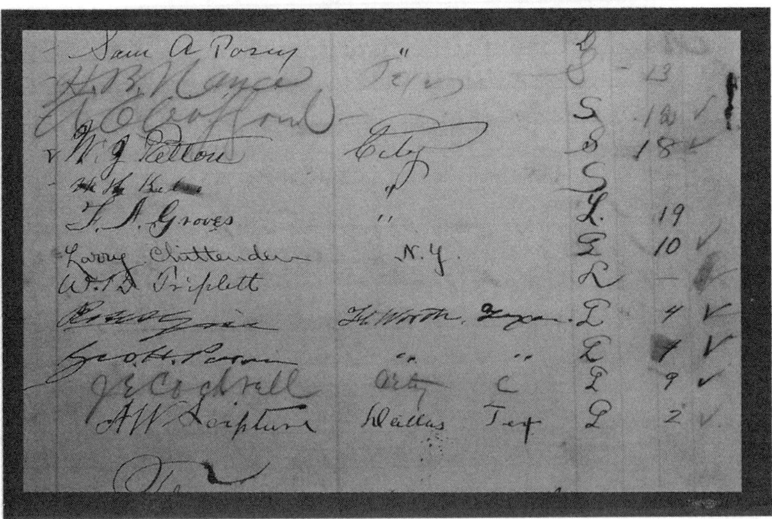

Sam A Posey

W. J. Pettoe — City — 18

T. A. Groves — 19

Larry Chittenden — N.Y. — 10

W. T. D. Triplett

Ft. Worth, Texas — 4

Geo. H. Parsons — 7

J E Cockrell — City — 9

A W Scipture — Dallas Tex — 2

Page and close-up of Larry Chittenden's signature in the Palace Hotel register in Abilene, Texas. Courtesy of John and Dolores Compere and Southwest Collection/Special Collections Library.

larger, ancestral family, something of a union between ancient Northern and Southern linages, were divided during the war, but his immediate family remained staunchly New York and New England Unionists. Nonetheless, Chittenden read Southern literature, especially novels by William Gilmore Simms of Charleston, and as a boy, according to at least one source, "He was always greatly interested in the romantic history of Texas and the heroes of the Alamo."[7]

Socially, the Chittenden family was well-connected in New York. Whatever prominence the Chittendens may have claimed was probably due to the great financial success of the family dry goods business, Henry Chittenden's role with Brooklyn's Plymouth Church, and Simeon Chittenden's position from 1873 to 1881 as a member of the New York legislature. In any case, the Chittendens were acquainted with members of the city's social and economic elite, and were often invited to major social events such as fancy balls or elaborate dinners.[8]

An older cousin, for example, Simeon Baldwin Chittenden—son of Larry's father's brother and business partner—was a highly successful real estate lawyer in Brooklyn and New York City. The younger Simeon was a member of such prestigious groups as the Rembrandt Club, the Hamilton Club, and the Brooklyn Chess Club, the latter of which was his favorite pastime. He loved the opera and fine paintings, and he spent as much of his free time as possible at Mapleside, the old Chittenden family home in Guilford, Connecticut, a place that had been in the family for ten generations. He gave liberally to libraries, hospitals, and other charities in New York and Brooklyn. More distant, and past, relatives, but also descendants of Guilford founder William Chittenden, included Thomas and Martin Chittenden, the first and eighth governors of Vermont.[9]

Perhaps for such reasons, the Chittendens became acquainted with members of the ranching and banking family headed by Swante Magnus Swenson. Swenson, a Swedish immigrant, had come to America in 1838 and for a time settled in the Austin, Texas. A successful merchant, he married into a Southern family with large plantations in Texas and Louisiana and owned slaves—although he personally abhorred the institution and fled to Mexico during the Civil War rather than fight for the Confederacy. Eventually, Swenson established a bank in New York City, but he maintained his mercantile business and expanded his land holdings in Texas. In the 1880s with his sons, Eric Pierson and Swen Alvin, and a nephew, Andrew, he began fencing portions of the Swenson Land and Cattle Company with its SMS brand in Jones and neighboring counties of West Texas.

Meanwhile, as a youth in Brooklyn, Larry Chittenden went to work in his father's and uncle's dry goods business, and as a result he grew up in the clothing industry. He learned to recognize and appreciate quality fabric, and the experience perhaps accounts for him as an adult always being nattily dressed. He did not buy his clothes "off the rack," one might say.

In 1880, when he was eighteen years old, Chittenden began reporting for New York newspapers—the *New York Herald* and the *New York Sun*—and local magazines. His older brother, Henry A. Chittenden, Jr., a well-known journalist for the *Herald* editorial staff was responsible for Larry's start. The work was part time, as his father and uncle kept him busy in their dry-goods company. Still, for three years, Chittenden sharpened his composition, improved his reporting techniques, and maintained his love of writing.[10]

Then at age twenty-one, Chittenden left New York. With an invitation from the Swenson brothers, Eric and Swen, to visit the ranch that they were fencing in Jones County, he borrowed fifty dollars from his uncle and headed for Texas. To provide a bit of additional income, he wrote about his travels for the *New York Herald* and other eastern newspapers and periodicals. He stopped in Saint Louis briefly before continuing southwestward with plenty of luggage to hold his carefully tailored clothes, outfits his cowboy friends found a bit unusual.[11] As an example, in 1883 at the first roundup he attended on the Swenson Land and Cattle Company's ranch (the Ericsdale) northeast of Anson, he was dressed, recalled one of the cowboys, in "a dark shirt and necktie. His trousers were tight fitting and stuffed into the tops of what looked to be race track boots."[12]

Chittenden did not stay long on the Swenson ranch. He examined the nearly ten thousand acres of ranch land northwest of Anson that his uncle, Simeon Chittenden, had purchased in 1882 from Swente Magnus Swenson. Then he toured the rolling prairie country of West Texas, stopping briefly in San Angelo. The record is not clear, but he may have returned to New York and Brooklyn to lobby his uncle into allowing him to oversee a West Texas cattle-raising operation on his uncle's nearly sixteen sections of land.

Simeon Chittenden was wealthy and restless. He had recently lost his bid for a fifth term for Congressman in the New York state House of Representatives and had retired from his Brooklyn-based clothing business. He was also generous. He gave tens of thousands of dollars to charities, in addition to nearly $240,000 to Yale University. Like many other eastern financiers, he got caught up in the booming Western land and cattle business, purchased some land, and, upon his nephew's favorable report, agreed to allow Larry Chittenden to supervise the Jones County enterprise.

In the early 1880s, cattle-raising was one of the hottest investments in the West, including Texas. Eastern and British capitalists formed huge "land and cattle" companies that came to control well over half the land and cattle in West Texas. The "companies," commonly referred to by their brands, included the JA, the Spur, the Pitchfork, the Four Sixes (6666), the Spade, the XIT, and Swenson's SMS, among others. The Matador Land and Cattle Company of Dundee, Scotland, one of the most successful ranching ventures in American history, in 1882 purchased 300,000 acres of land and 60,000 head of cattle. Its manager, Murdo Mackenzie, built the Matador until at its height it owned or leased some 1.6 million acres from Texas to Saskatchewan.

In the early 1880s, hundreds of people invested in the Texas range-cattle industry. It spread across the state with what some have called marvelous rapidity. Understandably, it was a booming business, for longhorn cattle purchased in Texas for five or six dollars a head were selling in Chicago and Cincinnati for thirty-five or forty dollars. In response, cowboys moved thousands of steers from Texas north along busy routes, such as the Chisholm Trail, to railroad centers in Abilene, Wichita, Ellsworth, and later Dodge City, Kansas. They also drove cattle, including cows and heifers, to Colorado, Wyoming, and the Dakotas to provide breeding stock to northern ranches. Indeed, drovers moved 60 percent of the longhorns beyond Kansas to northern ranches, military posts, and Indian reservations. Even a young Theodore Roosevelt invested in a large cattle operation in the North Dakota badlands.

The boom did not last. For every Murdo Mackenzie or Swante Magnus Swenson, or others, such as C. C. Slaughter or Charles Goodnight, who became a "cattle king," there were five others who lost their shirts or abandoned large-scale cattle raising altogether. The chief danger was overstocking ranges, which wrecked the grass and weakened cattle prices. Then, the increased use of barbed wire reduced the amount of grazing land: the XIT in West Texas, for instance, held an estimated six thousand miles of fence on its three million acres of land.

At the end of the 1880s, cattle raising in Texas was ceasing to be a frontier way of life. The Chisholm Trail was virtually closed, and traffic on other trails

Larry Chittenden ranch house in Jones County, c. 1890s. Courtesy of Texas Cowboys' Christmas Ball Association.

was tapering off. Then, a hard drought in the summer of 1886 sandwiched between catastrophic winters in 1885–1886 and 1886–1887 brought significant changes to the Texas industry. Many cattlemen went broke in the late 1880s and early 1890s, sold out, and left the once-booming enterprise. Those who survived the environmental and economic bust transformed Texas and Great Plains ranching, turning it from something of an adventure to a settled, carefully managed business. Although it was ephemeral, the cattle frontier in the West, as some have called the open range era, by its sheer majestic grandeur continues to capture the imagination of people everywhere.[13]

Larry Chittenden joined the cattle-raising industry before the bust. He convinced his wealthy, restless uncle to purchase cattle for the recently acquired ranch and thus become part of the land and livestock adventure. Together the neophyte cattlemen from New York jumped into ranching on the open range land at the foot of Skinout Mountain about eight miles northwest of Anson. They employed a general manager, hired ranch hands, and fenced the ranch. After completing the fencing, they brought in the common Texas cattle breed (a crossbred mix of Iberian longhorn and southern cattle), bought horses, and established a brand, the SBC.

The two ranching novices found that some wild horses, or mustangs,

Larry Chittenden's room inside his ranch house, c. 1890s. Courtesy of Texas Cowboys' Christmas Ball Association.

that grazed their ranch's uplands had been enclosed within the barbed wire borders of their property. Their cowboys tamed a couple of the horses, sold some of them, and released the others.

The Chittenden Ranch, as Larry Chittenden named it, and its SBC brand survived the environmental and economic woes of the mid-1880s and afterwards. When market forces in the East demanded better beef than the tough, lean longhorn meat, the Chittendens followed the Swenson example and brought in purebred Herefords and Durhams (shorthorns) to improve the meat quality of their animals. A couple of years later, Larry Chittenden was among the first local ranchers to introduce polled, black Aberdeen Angus to Jones County and the north central section of Texas.[14]

Not all was pleasant. Cattle prices remained low for years after the industry collapse in the late 1880s and drought remained a recurring problem. In fact, in the 1890s several cattlemen moved to divide their property into smaller pieces and sell sections to farmers or farmer-stockmen. Then, in 1889, Simeon Chittenden died. Although saddened by the news, a determined Larry Chittenden stayed on the ranch and on June 2, 1890, purchased the property from his uncle's estate. Chittenden paid $37,000 for the nearly sixteen square miles of property, or roughly $3.50 an acre.[15]

At the time, Larry Chittenden was well-dressed, well-read, and financially successful. He was the twenty-eight-year-old proprietor of a large Jones County ranch. He was thoughtful, reserved, and kind-hearted. He has been called "a man of rare mental powers, keen observation and vast worldly experience, yet modest and natural withal." A contemporary, F. S. Brittain, described him in the *Abilene Reporter* as "a slight, well-built, active, youngish man, with a well-shaped head of wavy, glossy black hair, [and a] black mustache." He had "a face browned by out-of-door life, with a nose that seems as sensitively full of life as that of a well-bred terrier, and a mouth both strong and sweet, the whole lit up by a pair of changeable eyes, now gray, now blue, ever moving and full of interest." He was a gracious host, according to Hybernia Grace, "but as a rule [he] avoided social gatherings."[16]

An exceptional athlete who had always enjoyed outdoor activities, Chittenden became a skilled horseman. He rode with his ranch hands in roundups and across the range, and he spent time hunting with several different Jones County friends, but particularly with John Milsap. An excellent swimmer and remarkable diver, according to one source, "he saved two women from drowning in the surf at Spring Lake, [New Jersey,] in 1891, and a man from drowning at Barbados" in the West Indies in 1906.[17]

On his ranch, Chittenden continued to raise cattle, of course, but he also began to farm. His men cultivated two hundred acres on a lowland prairie section of the ranch. They planted feed crops, such as grain sorghum, in the early years of the agricultural experiment but in the late 1890s turned to raising winter wheat. They planted the wheat in the late summer or early fall, and after it had grown a few inches and before the first hard freeze, they could graze cattle on the green shoots. In the spring, the wheat usually returned unharmed and Chittenden's employees could harvest it late in the spring. Grazing cattle on his winter wheat from December to early March helped to preserve his grasslands. He also raised about two hundred horses and mules.

Obviously, employees on the ranch came and went. Many were young men who sought work for a time before trying their own ranching or farming venture. One such person was Will Fomby, one of the first settlers in Jones County's Wise Chapel community. He gained experience as a cow hand, according to Shelton and Hutto, "when he went on a trail drive with a herd of Larry Chittenden cattle."[18] He probably herded the animals to Abilene, which after the arrival of a railroad became an important livestock shipping point. But, he may have been with Charles H. Tompkins and other cowboys who moved a herd of Chittenden's cattle from Gaines County, to where Chittenden had moved them on account of short grass during the drought years in the early 1890s, back to the Jones County ranch.[19]

A number of other cowhands are singled out in Chittenden's "Returning to the Ranch" published in *Bermuda Verses* (or "Gettin' Back to the Ranch," as it is titled in later editions of *Ranch Verses*). The poem describes one of his fall arrivals back at his ranch. In its second stanza he writes:

> I've seen a heap uv pleasant things, and yet it did me good
> To spy ole Jim in his ole jeans just packin' in the wood!
> An' thar wuz Buck an' Horseshoe Sam, an thar up the sill,
> All smiles an' spurs an' high-heeled boots, wuz rustler, Windy Bill.
> Oh, Bill, they say, has got renown, an' perhaps you may recall
> How he performed one Christmas time an' led the "Cowboys' Ball."

Chittenden mentions a couple of other hands in the lively, sixty-two-line poem, including one named "John" and another named "Gash Knife," apparently a nickname for a cowhand who had recently worked for the Hash Knife outfit in Taylor County. He also indicates that Windy Bill was the ranch cook.[20]

Chittenden built a small, wood-frame house on the property and promptly turned most of the home over to his ranch manager and his family. An old photo of the house shows a broad, covered porch along the entire front of the structure, and above the porch a sign reading "Chittenden Ranch" is attached. A buffalo skull sits over the sign. A tall yard fence of wood and barbed wire surrounds the front of the comfortable building, and the manager or his wife maintained well-kept flower beds.

Chittenden kept one room in the house for himself. It was a comfortable little combination bedroom, office, and writing area on the building's southeast corner and looked out on Skinout Mountain. Simply but richly furnished, according to Hybernia Grace, it was a reflection of the ranch owner. She notes, "The walls were covered with rare pictures, and photographs of friends from all parts of the world." She further writes that "[s]nake skins and rattles, horns and guns strangely mingled with fans and lace scarfs." Also in the room, Chittenden kept a library of over nine hundred carefully selected books.[21]

Skinout Mountain. Courtesy of Monte L. Monroe.

In the tightly packed, but cozy little room Chittenden spent much of his time while on the ranch. He worked on articles and stories for New York newspapers and wrote his ranch poetry. He climbed the Skinout highlands from where he enjoyed "an inspiring and delightful view" of the countryside, including the Double Mountains in Stonewall County. On the Skinout he might spend many hours in the shade of a mesquite tree working on his cowboy poetry. In a burst of romantic exaggeration Grace writes, "The fragrance of the Texas wild flowers, the songs of birds, the invigorating fresh air which Chittenden enjoyed from this inspiration point—all this together with the solitude of the prairies inspired him to write."[22]

One of Chittenden's first Texas poems appeared in the *San Angelo Standard.* Published there in 1885 and, according to Grace, "inspired by a beautiful San Angelo girl," the little piece was titled "The Odd Fellow's Ball." Apparently, the work impressed his father who "praised the poem highly." Indeed, his father, who once opposed his son's dabbling in literature, upon reading the poem, "encouraged his son to continue his writing."[23]

One of the first poems he wrote in Jones County was titled "My Old Friend, 'The Majah Green.'" Written in the spring of 1888 and printed in the local newspaper, the *Texas Western,* it describes an early Anson resident from the South who had fought in the Civil War for the Confederacy, earning the rank of major. If our poet is honest with his verse, Green and Chittenden spent much time together, hunting and riding across western Jones County. Green was a storyteller who around evening camp fires related stories of his youth and the Civil War.[24]

There were many other poems of course. The most famous of them is "The Cowboys' Christmas Ball." Its story has been told in any number of magazines and newspapers. Although set in 1885, it really describes two or three Christmas-time dances Chittenden attended at the Star Hotel. A lively, catchy poem of 144 lines it represents, as Michael Hoinski writes, "a burst of lyricism . . . in vernacular grandiosity." When read aloud or sung, it is enjoyable, charming, and easy to listen to.[25]

Chittenden gathered many of his poems, carried them to the offices of G. P. Putnam's Sons in New York, and sought their publication. In 1893, the venerable, old book company printed *Ranch Verses*, a collection of 133 poems by the soon to be self-styled "Poet-Ranchman" of Texas. The 5" x 8" book with a dark brown cover contains neither an introduction nor a preface in its 189 pages, but Chittenden writes on the title page that "the verses in this little volume are offspring of solitude—born in idle hours on a Texas ranch." The poems begin immediately after the table of contents and a short list of illustrations. The poems cover a wide range of topics and several relate to ranching and life in the cattle and farming frontier of northwest Texas. Several of the poems describe the sea, the Maine coast, and sailing, but many of them are about young women, suggesting perhaps that the unmarried writer was a love-sick poet. A few poems are devoted to his ancestral family, friends, New York, or his Montclair birthplace. The photos show various ranching and sea-side scenes.

The book with its unsophisticated frontier vernacular was an immediate success. G. P. Putnam's Sons ran second and third printings almost immediately and additional printings within a few years. Then, in 1898 the publisher issued another printing, something of a revised and enlarged edition. The 133 poems remained the same, and in the same 1893 order, but the cover now was green with "Poet Ranchman" beneath the poet's name. A bigger change, apparently, and the one that allowed the publisher to call it a new edition, was the addition of five pages at the end of the book containing in small print "A Selection of Fifty Press Opinions of 'Ranch Verses.' "

The review clippings are, of course, highly complimentary of the book—even those from Europe, where the book sold well. The *London Saturday*

Review, for example, suggested that the verses "are tuneful, manly in sentiment and musical in flow. They have a right cheerful tone, and are full of spirit and vivacity." The *New York Press* reviewer wrote that *Ranch Verses* is one "of the most interesting and readable books of poetry ever published," and the reviewer for the *Boston Literary World* said, "*Ranch Verses* have a swing and dash and a rare freshness." And, then, there is Chittenden's brother's paper, the *New York Herald*. Its reviewer said, "Mr. Chittenden has done his work carefully. . . . [W]e feel that ranch life has a good deal that is enticing in it when we read such lines as 'The Cowboys' Christmas Ball.' "[26]

Chittenden published poems in several places. They were printed in such Texas newspapers as the *Abilene Reporter*, the Anson *Texas Western*, the *Dallas Morning News*, the *Houston Post*, the *Galveston Daily News*, and the *San Angelo Standard*. Magazines and newspapers in New York and New Jersey found a place for the poems, and in fact they appeared in periodicals throughout the country. And his book, of course, sold well with new printings and new editions coming out nearly every year during the first twelve years after its release. At the time of Chittenden's death in 1934, *Ranch Verses* was in its sixteenth edition.

Ranch Verses was not Chittenden's only book of poetry. While living for a time in Bermuda after 1904 Chittenden worked on a second collection, and in 1909 G. P. Putnam's Sons published *Bermuda Verses*. One of the poems in *Bermuda Verses* is titled "Lafferty's Bermuda Letter." It was popular enough that some people asserted Chittenden wrote an entire book entitled *Lafferty's Letters*.[27] No such book has yet been located. *Bermuda Verses* did not enjoy the great success of his first volume. Indeed, in 2013, owners of a first edition of *Ranch Verses* were asking three hundred dollars for their little book, one in only fair condition.

Larry Chittenden must be considered one of the early cowboy poets. Cowboys, granted, for years had been strumming ditties around trail-drive camp fires, and on night-herding duty they had long been singing gentle tunes to calm the animals they were watching. Some of their song lyrics made their way into print before Chittenden's publication in 1893. Nonetheless, *Ranch Verses*, which was widely read in the South and East and in the western cattle country, may have inspired an entire generation of younger cowboys to try their hand at versifying. By the late-twentieth century cowboy poetry conferences had become popular and widespread, and cowboy poetry the subject of serious scholarly study.

Some critics have called Chittenden's poetry doggerel, and clearly his society (i.e., playful) verse, which "hardly rises above the ordinary," borders on triviality. One of his harshest early critics was John A. Lomax, the collector of range and ranch folk songs. Lomax writes that Chittenden has three types of poetry in *Ranch Verses*: society, moralizing or didactic, and ranch verse. There is, writes Lomax, "considerable unevenness in his work." He lacks both technical skill and genius to make his playful verse give pleasure, argues Lomax, and many poems reflect mediocrity. Plus, he "has put a good deal of 'Way Down East' dialect into the mouths of his cowpunchers."[28]

Other reviewers are less critical. Some suggest Chittenden's farm and ranch poems with their refreshing breeziness show poetic ability, and his descriptive cow country poems, especially those that use a western ranch dialect, such as "The Cowboy's Christmas Ball" and "Gettin' Back to the Ranch," are musical, graceful, and clever. Much of Chittenden's poetry is practical and descriptive of ranch life, including its roundups, amusements, and hardships. A number of early reviewers gushed that his poetry surpassed that of Bret Harte and Joaquin Miller, and one reviewer suggested that his poetry, at least in the poem "Hidden," was worthy of Alfred Tennyson or Henry Wadsworth Longfellow.[29]

If David Foute Eagleton is correct, Chittenden's poetry is typical of Texas literature before the turn of the century—"a reflection of life of the people." Two features stand out in such literature, Eagleton argues, and both are strikingly characteristic of Chittenden's verse: "their love of the natural beauty about them; and their intense, passionate affection and loyalty for the land of their birth or adoption."[30] As Nola McKey writes, Chittenden's poetry is remarkable "for its description and artful portrayal of frontier life."[31] Some might argue that Chittenden was little more than a rhymer and not always a good one.

Walter Prescott Webb, writing in *The Great Plains*, said poetry associated with "the cattle kingdom," as he called it, fell into two classes: "the conscious literary effort of the poets of the West and the folk poetry." Most of the "conscious poetry," Webb wrote, was "of mediocre quality and destined for oblivion." Such cowboy poets as Larry Chittenden, Webb noted, "perhaps made the best contributions" to the poetry of the cattle kingdom. "The Cowboys' Christmas Ball," Webb suggested, "promises to live as a part of the more poetic folklore of the Plains Country."[32]

After the great critical and economic success of *Ranch Verses*, Chittenden

Double Mountain. Courtesy of Monte L. Monroe.

began attending some of the literary salons in the East. He visited his family in Montclair and New York, purchased a summer cottage in Connecticut along Long Island Sound, and hung out there with several literary friends. Although shy, he was popular, a gracious host, and a wonderful storyteller. His athletic ability, combined with his money and success, gave him confidence, attracted people to him, and made him many friends. Like his father, uncle, and older cousin, however, he was careful about his finances.[33]

Each fall before 1904, Chittenden returned to the Jones County ranch. He renewed his friendships with people in Anson, joined his cowhands with work on the ranch, and dabbled with poetry and other writing—newspaper essays, for example. He hunted and went camping. He climbed the uplands of Skinout Mountain and there spent much time in solitude writing poetry and singing songs.

Then, beginning in 1904, rather than returning to the ranch, he spent several winters in Bermuda. He bought or built a large home a few miles from Hamilton, the capital, and called the place Larry's Lodge. The home was a large white house with a steep roof and a long, covered front porch that faced out toward Church Bay in Harrington Sound. Five steps led up to the porch, whose nearly flat roof, in contrast to the rest of the home, extended the length of the building and six large pillars supported the roof. The interior of the house contained high ceilings and furniture crowded the rooms. The walls were painted white, but, like the little room in his ranch house, they were covered with photos and paintings. A fireplace stood in the living area and books lined shelves in several rooms.[34]

Here Chittenden enjoyed life, spending much of his time swimming in the surf, playing tennis, and sometimes working on his poetry. In 1909, G. P. Putnam's Sons published *Bermuda Verses.* A little book, it contained twenty-four poems in sixty-eight pages plus five pages of "A Selection of Fifty Press Opinions of 'Ranch Verses.'" Chittenden dedicated the book "To all lovers of Bermuda."

Although it was the capital of Bermuda, Hamilton was a small community. Tourism and government services represented its major industries, but the city was also the largest and most important port for Bermuda. Americans filled the hotels and streets of Hamilton, especially during the winter months, and Chittenden visited many of them.

In fact, a good number of friends from New York and New England visited Chittenden in Bermuda. Most of his visitors took a train to the South Carolina or Georgia coast. From there they boarded a boat for Hamilton, and upon arrival at the capital city they rode in a buggy or wagon to Larry's Lodge. A few people hired a driver and an automobile and took the new-fashioned vehicle out to the popular home.[35]

Chittenden did not stay permanently in Bermuda. He continued to travel. He went to his Jones County ranch on several occasions to renew his cowboy friendships, check on his property, and oversee repairs as needed, and each summer he continued to visit various resorts in the New Jersey-New York-New England area. In the spring of 1914, he was in Europe when World War I broke out, causing him a number of inconveniences before he could return to America.

Back in the United States, Chittenden promoted American participation in World War I on the side of England, France, and their allies. He was loyal and patriotic but, as he was fifty-five years old when the United States entered the war in 1917, he did not serve. Still, some of the poems he wrote during the crucial years between 1914 and 1918 reflect his patriotism.[36]

In the 1920s, Chittenden invested in Florida real estate. As with many other Americans he got caught up in the great "Florida land boom" in the early to mid-1920s. By 1926, when the boom became a bust, the population of Florida had doubled. Some people had bought land sight unseen or paid for real estate that was a foot underwater. Chittenden was more fortunate. He purchased property and built a vacation home in Palm Beach and held additional property in West Palm Beach.[37]

In 1921, Larry Chittenden opened another library. He started "The Autograph Library," as he called it, in his home, which he named "The Sea Bird's Nest." It was located in Christmas Cove, Lincoln County, Maine, a place he made his summer home from late June to mid-September every year in the 1920s. The village of Christmas Cove, located on Rutherford Island, was in 2013 part of the town South Bristol. In the 1920s and early 1930s, few people lived there most of the year, but in the summer visitors packed its resort hotels and many permanent residents accepted vacationers in their homes.

Many book lovers and literary types, including Chittenden, vacationed at Christmas Cove (also the name of a long narrow bay) or spent the summer there. After Chittenden started his library, having purchased many of the books himself, summer visitors contributed hundreds of volumes. Several special "corners," such as The Clergyman's Corner, The Texas Corner, and the Maine Corner, appeared as people gave, respectively, books on religion, Texas, or Maine to the library. The Children's Corner included more than a thousand books devoted to needs and desires of children and adolescents. It was Chittenden's special nook, and children using the library called him "Uncle Larry."[38]

The original library was unusual. Founded, developed, and maintained by Chittenden, it opened each June 20, shortly after the poet ranchman arrived. Before the library closed in the fall, each permanent family of Christmas Cove could check out up to fifty books. Family members returned the books nine months later when the library opened again in June. No books were lost during the first decade of its unusual operation. Chittenden charged no fees, dues, or fines, and he paid all costs for the library until his death in 1934.[39]

Chittenden died September 24, 1934, in New York City of complications resulting from surgery. He was seventy-two years old. Elizabeth E. Pinkham, his sister and only surviving sibling, buried him at the family plot in Rosedale Cemetery in Montclair, New Jersey. He never married, and as a result, he had no children to whom he might have bequeathed his estate. In his will, much like his father and uncle, he provided that any funds remaining in his estate after probate be distributed to some forty-two individuals and charities.[40]

William Lawrence "Larry" Chittenden was generous, innovative, restless, and always interesting. He loved the Texas ranch country, but he also enjoyed Bermuda, his home in Florida, and the resorts in Connecticut, New York, and Maine. He was a marvelous athlete, an intellectual, a reporter, and a poet of great renown, who, unlike most poets, saw his first book of poetry go through twelve printings in its first twelve years after publication. He made a living from his ranch and from his cowboy poetry, much of which he created on his Jones County property near where in 1885, by happenstance, he "went to that reception, 'The Cowboys' Christmas Ball.' " Not long afterward, Jones County, Texas, became his winter home.

Chapter Four

Explicating Chittenden's Popular Poem

Larry Chittenden came to Texas and Jones County in 1883. He attended his first Anson western dance party during the Christmas season in 1885, and he wrote "The Cowboys' Christmas Ball" after attending one or two additional Christmas-time dances.[1] According to the author, the happenings in the popular ballad occurred in 1885, perhaps the year M. G. Rhoads and his wife first staged a dance. At the time, Anson and Jones County lay on the western edge of Anglo settlement, and Anson served as the county's political, judicial, and administrative seat.[2]

Chittenden's famous poem sits solidly in contemporary nineteenth-century western America and West Texas literary traditions. That is, literature, including poetry, produced along the line of settlement, or "frontier" as University of Wisconsin historian Frederick Jackson Turner called the westward advancing zone, was American in subject, theme, and style. Rather than imitate European forms, it was a reflection of the life and work of the people of Texas and America. In many ways, like Texas music, Texas literature reflects a crossroads, a meeting place, of Western and Southern traditions. In the nineteenth century, Texas literature was written for and about pioneer neighbors, many of whom could trace their ancestry back through East Texas and the Old South to Virginia and ultimately to southern England. In a sense, as one critic writes, literature of western Texas in the 1880s was "indigenous to the soil."[3]

Such at least was the case with Chittenden's "The Cowboys' Christmas Ball." As noted previously, the poem appeared first in Hec McEachern's

Larry Chittenden, c. 1900. Courtesy of Anson–Jones Museum.

Anson newspaper the *Texas Western* in 1890, and it gained national attention after 1893 when the New York publishing house G. P Putnam's Sons printed a collection of Chittenden's poems under the title *Ranch Verses*. The book went through sixteen printings before Chittenden's death in 1934, but just as importantly the famous poem, as Becky Davidson writes, left to posterity "a written record of the social and economic status of a small town" in a growing, but still something of a pioneer, county of northwest Texas.[4]

Again, by describing a popular event in Anson and by using the names of local citizens, the poem falls squarely in contemporary traditions of American frontier and early Great Plains literature.[5] Chittenden's use of simple rhymes, a catchy iambic meter, and the colloquial but colorful language of 1880s West Texas contributed to the poem's popularity. Indeed, the poem plus Anson and Jones County traditions led, in the 1930s, to an annual revival of the dance the poem describes.

Cowboys sang versions of Chittenden's ballad before the turn of the century. N. Howard "Jack" Thorp, for example, included the verse in his *Songs of the Cowboys*, published in 1908, but he writes that he learned of the "song" from a "Miss Jessi Forbes, at Eddy, New Mexico in 1898." Likewise, before 1910, John A. Lomax, who collected cowboy poetry and music, had heard the piece sung around a New Mexico campfire, and he included the poem in his 1916 edition of *Cowboy Songs and Other Frontier Ballads.*[6]

More recently, performers such as Michael Martin Murphey have performed music versions of the poem. Murphey, a Grammy Award–winning artist, recorded the song in 1985. In late 2011, The Killers, a Las Vegas rock band, not only recorded a spoof of the music and words of Chittenden's poem, but also released a video (made available on the Web) of a Christmas-themed spaghetti western set in Las Vegas and based on the music and lyrics.[7]

Here, then, is William Lawrence "Larry" Chittenden's 1880s poem as it appeared in the first edition of *Ranch Verses* (1893). After each of the six stanzas an explanation of the people and events cited in it follows. The people, many of whom were friends and companions of Chittenden, attended the dances. The events the author describes, such as the "pulling of the badger" in the second stanza, occurred; several of them, such as the howling of the coyotes in the first stanza, obviously were common in the greater West.

First Stanza

'Way out in Western Texas, where the Clear Fork's waters flow,
Where the cattle are "a-browzin'," an' the Spanish ponies grow;
Where the Northers "come a-whistlin'" from beyond the Neutral strip;
And the prairie dogs are sneezin', as if they had "The Grip";
Where the cayotes come a-howlin' 'round the ranches after dark,
And the mocking-birds are singin' to the lovely "medder lark";
Where the 'possum and the badger, and rattlesnakes abound,
And the monstrous stars are winkin' o'er a wilderness profound;
Where lonesome, tawny prairies melt into airy streams,
Where the Double Mountains slumber, in heavenly kinds of dreams;
Where the antelope is grazin' and the lonely plovers call—
It was there that I attended "The Cowboys' Christmas Ball."

The first stanza establishes the setting. Chittenden places the dance in West Texas, near the Clear Fork of the Brazos River in Jones County. The Double Mountains in neighboring Stonewall County could be seen from the top of Skinout Mountain, the long, low mesa at the edge of the Chittenden Ranch.

John Milsap, c. 1890.
Courtesy of Texas Cowboys' Christmas Ball Association.

The Double Mountains served as a favorite landmark for Apaches, Comanches, and other Native Americans. It likewise was an important guide for Anglo explorers, soldiers, bison hunters, cattle trailers, and others passing through the unpopulated region.

The Clear Fork branch of the Brazos River (Rio Los Brazos de Dios) rises in Scurry County. It moves through Fisher County above Roby, and flows eastward in Jones County below Anson and turns abruptly northward to exit the county near Lueders. It joins the main stream of the Brazos in Young County just above Possum Kingdom Lake. With its tributaries, the Clear Fork is the major drainage system of Jones County.

Chittenden likewise makes note of the region's prairie topography, its clear, cloudless skies full of nighttime stars, and its expansive open landscape with water-filled streams and plenty of ranches. The reference to the Neutral strip refers to non-Indian land in Oklahoma Territory north of Texas, and "Northers" was a Texas term used to describe a cold wind or cool breeze blowing southward down the Great Plains.

The author also writes about the area's ubiquitous wildlife, including prairie dogs, coyotes, opossums, badgers, antelope, and rattlesnakes. He mentions mocking birds, meadowlarks, and plovers but no game birds, such as prairie chickens, grouse, and doves. Reminiscences of early settlers and Jones County histories support Chittenden's wildlife reporting. H. C. Carr spoke "of thousands of antelope" in the county "in the late 1870s and early 1880s." Carr, writes Becky Davidson, "also spoke of the large number of prairie dogs, turkey, deer, and . . . mountain lions," plus wolves and black bears.[8]

Finally in the first stanza, Chittenden makes an effort to contrast East and West. He intersperses local speech forms of the West with something of an eastern "cultured style" he brought with him from New York in 1883. By such writing, he attempts to integrate for the poem's readers the diverse and distant sections of the country.[9]

Second Stanza

The town was Anson City, old Jones's county seat,
Where they raise Polled Angus cattle, and waving whiskered wheat;
Where the air is soft and "bammy," an' dry an' full of health,
And the prairies is explodin' with agricultural wealth;
Where they print the *Texas Western*, that Hec. McCann supplies,
With news and yarns and stories, of most amazin' size;
Where Frank Smith "pulls the badger," on knowin' tenderfeet,
And Democracy's triumphant, and mighty hard to beat;
Where lives that good old hunter, John Milsap from Lamar,
Who "used to be the Sheriff, back East, in Paris sah!"
'T was there, I say, at Anson, with the lively "Wider Wall,"
That I went to that reception, "The Cowboys' Christmas Ball."

The second stanza adds additional background information, but now it relates more to Anson than to Jones County. Chittenden notes that Anson is the county seat and that the community's economic viability is based on agriculture, especially on growing wheat and raising cattle. The reference to polled Angus cattle is interesting because Chittenden, who operated a ranch near Skinout Mountain, a mesa about seven miles northwest of Anson, was perhaps the first person, as Becky Davidson writes, "to bring the breed to that area of Texas."[10] The Hec McCann reference is to Hec McEachern who was the editor and publisher of the Anson newspaper. As noted previously,

Dick Davis had begun the *Texas Western* in 1883, but by 1885 McEachern had taken over its operation.

Frank Smith, a popular and lively character, owned a general merchandise business in Anson and opened a bank in his store. In an undated letter written by Mrs. Lucien Keene, daughter of the owner of the Star Hotel, Smith is described as a "good chess player and an entertainer with his music."[11] He was also a practical joker. The Chittenden line that says Smith "pulls the badger" refers to a prank common in rural, newly settled areas. The trick was often played on newcomers, especially those who might have enough money in their pocket to buy a round of drinks afterward.

The prank could be a bit complicated. The group planning the joke needed a good sport as well as someone with some pocket change. As explained by several chroniclers, after finding a useful dupe, or "tenderfoot," the group began talking about a dog and badger fight and making bets as to the winner of the dog versus badger encounter, a fight that would last until one of the contestants was dead. They then talked about who should serve as referee, that is, the person who, using a rope tied around the badger's neck, must pull the wild creature out of the barrel or covered tub in which he was being held. Next they turned to the newcomer, suggesting that because he did not have money invested in the fight's outcome, he ought to pull the badger. He usually agreed.

Thereupon the group headed for the place, usually behind a building but sometimes in an empty, unused room, where the barrel was located. The men brought along a dog, of course, to add to the charade, and as they walked to the appointed spot, they gave the "referee" advice on how to pull the rope most effectively. When all was ready, the unsuspecting newcomer braced himself and with rope in hand pulled hard. Instead of a badger, out came a bucket of slop from the local restaurant or a hotel chamber pot with sometimes the contents splashing everywhere. The perpetrators burst into laughter, and all headed for the local saloon or other place where refreshments could be found.[12]

John Milsap, as the poem notes, was a sheriff in Paris, Lamar County, Texas, before moving to Jones County in 1883. The Milsap family settled near what became Neinda, which was located north and west of Chittenden's Skinout Mountain ranch, and John and Chittenden were frequent hunting partners. Milsap, his wife, and their six children may all have attended the Star Hotel dances in the 1880's, including the first one in 1884 or 1885. If so, the Milsap family's experience might indicate that the poem represented an amalgamation of two or three Christmas dances at the Star Hotel. Moreover, Chittenden did not give the poem to editor McEachern until 1889 or, more likely, 1890, and thus "it was probably not completed until a short time before" McEachern received it. Remember, it was first published on June 16, 1890.[13]

The "Wider Wall" reference remains a bit confusing. Because Hooper Shelton and Homer Hutto in their book on the history of Jones County make no mention of a Wall family, the term probably has to do with folks sitting on benches or chairs at the edge of the dance floor or in an adjoining room. Chittenden, a shy person, was a bit of a loner who never married, and, perhaps, he is indicating that, having come to the dance alone, he was something of a wallflower.

Third Stanza

The boys had left the ranches and come to town in piles;
The ladies—"kinder scatterin' "—had gathered in for miles.
And yet the place was crowded, as I remember well,
'T was got for the occasion, at "The Morning Star Hotel."
The music was a fiddle an' a lively tambourine,
And a "viol come imported," by the stage from Abilene.
The room was togged out gorgeous—with mistletoe and shawls,
And candles flickered frescoes, around the airy walls.
The "wimmin folks" looked lovely—the boys looked kinder treed,
Till their leader commenced yellin': "Whoa! fellers, let's stampede,"
And the music started sighin', and awailin' through the hall,
As a kind of introduction to "The Cowboys' Christmas Ball."

Much of the information in the third stanza is not new to this chapter. As noted earlier, for instance, some party guests to West Texas dances traveled considerable distance, a few from seventy or eighty miles away—which could mean a two- or three-day ride to the dance. They came on horseback, in buggies, wagons, and buckboards. As Chittenden notes, some came to Anson on the stagecoach. Also, anyone who heard or read about the dance "considered himself invited."[14] Likewise, such balls were often staged in honor of a newly married couple, who led the grand march, held near Christmas or New Year's

William "Windy Bill" Wilkinson, a cowboy, was the quadrille caller at the 1885 Christmas dance at the Star Hotel. Courtesy of Texas Cowboys' Christmas Ball Association.

Eve, or performed during a Fourth of July celebration, which was one of the most popular holidays in the West.

Large rooms in which to hold such balls were hard to find. The dances were sometimes held in a ranch bunkhouse or, if in a county seat town, often the courthouse. In the third stanza, Chittenden notes that the dining room at Rhoads' hotel was crowded, owing perhaps to a combination of the room's small size and the large number of people in attendance. Mrs. Lucien Keene, daughter of the Star Hotel's owners, in an undated letter to Leonora Barrett, organizer and first historian of the 1934 reenactment of "The Cowboys' Christmas Ball," indicated that the hotel's dining room even with the tables removed held space for only two sets of square dancers. She wrote, "The room was lighted by two swinging lamps with white shades at each end of the room and a chandelier holding two lamps in the center." She noted, but did not clearly remember, if "some branches of mistletoe were twined into the lamps."[15]

In the poem, Chittenden writes of three musicians providing the dance music. There may have been four. The big bass viol, presumably with its player, came in on the stage from Abilene, and apparently Chittenden was on the same stage. Someone played a tambourine, and two brothers, Clarence and Walter Wright of Roby, played fiddles.[16] There was no drummer, of course, nor keyboard player.

Everybody dressed up for the dance. New or just-cleaned shirts and polished boots for men were common. Rhoads allowed no spurs on the boots in his hotel, and men removed their hats in the presence of women. The women, according to Mrs. Keene, altered their dresses a bit to make them festive. Some may have sewed ruffles to the neckline. But many people attending dances such as Anson's 1885 Christmas ball could not afford special clothes for a wedding or the receptions that might follow. The same was true of a "big blowout" such as that at the Star Hotel, but nonetheless guests and hosts prepared well in advance.[17]

Fourth Stanza

The leader was a fellow that came from Swenson's Ranch,
They called him "Windy Billy," from "little Deadman's Branch."
His rig was "kinder keerless," big spurs and high-heeled boots;
He had the reputation that comes when "fellers shoots,"
His voice was like a bugle upon the mountain's height;
His feet were animated, an' a *mighty movin' sight,*
When he commenced to holler, "Neow, fellers, stake yer pen!
"Lock horns ter all them heifers, an' russle 'em like men.
"Saloot yer lovely critters; neow swing an' let 'em go,
"Climb the grape vine 'round 'em—all hands do-ce-do!
"You Mavericks, jine the round-up—Jest skip her waterfall,"
Huh! hit wuz gettin' active, "The Cowboys' Christmas Ball!"

The Swenson Ranch mentioned in the fourth stanza sprawled across many miles of Jones, Throckmorton, Stonewall, and adjoining counties. It began, perhaps, in 1854 when Swante Magnus Swenson, a Swedish immigrant living in Austin, invested in a Texas railway company, an investment that gained him 100,000 acres in north and northwest Texas. Then in the early 1880s Swenson redeemed railroad script for 500 sections (320,000 acres) of land in the Jones-Throckmorton area and began to fence the range and stock it with cattle. The subsequent SMS Ranching syndicate was huge, and in the early twentieth century, it purchased the Espuela (Spur) Land and Cattle Company and established the towns of Spur (in Dickens County) and Swenson (in Stonewall County).[18]

Windy Billy, or William Wilkinson, lived on the Swenson Ranch, called the Eleonora, in Throckmorton County. His childhood was difficult, and perhaps as a result he grew up edgy, willful, and a bit wild. Note, for example, that against hotel rules Chittenden has Bill wearing spurs in the building, and, reportedly, he once rode his horse up the stairs in the Star Hotel. According to his youngest daughter and her husband, after his mother died, Bill's father left him and his sister with a friend and his wife in Fort Worth while he went looking for work. Bill never saw his father again.[19]

When he was still a youth, Bill accompanied his new "guardian" to the Fort Worth stockyards where the man worked. While there cowboys from a Swenson ranch, probably the one in Williamson County, delivered a herd of cattle. The foreman of the Swenson outfit, or so the story goes, remarked favorably on Bill, and the guardian, seeing a chance to free himself of his responsibilities for the boy, talked about Bill's situation. The two men agreed that Bill should accompany the foreman back to the Swenson ranch. It was done. And, Bill, who began work by following a ranch chuck wagon, soon became a six-year-old cowboy—a "cow boy" indeed.[20]

Perhaps he lived along Deadman's Creek for a time, but in the 1880s he joined the newly established Swenson ranch near Throckmorton. He worked on a number of other spreads as well, including the Chittenden Ranch, and in the late 1880s, about the time the poem was being written, he worked for the Call Barr Ranch, headquartered in Stonewall County.[21]

The "little Deadman's Branch" phrase refers to Deadman Creek. The tiny stream rises in Callahan County, moves northwest into Jones County, and turns north to run parallel to the Jones-Shackelford county line before emptying into the Clear Fork of the Brazos River. About thirty miles long, the creek became known by its present name after a man was found dead at one of its crossings.[22]

Some of the language in the fourth stanza is troublesome. Mrs. Lucien Keene, daughter of the Star Hotel's owners, suggested that most men in the 1880s while in the presence of ladies would not refer to young women as "heifers" or "critters." According to Becky Davidson, Mrs. Keene wrote that "Southern chivalry would not have permitted a [dance] caller to" use the terms in such a public way. Men, obviously, used such terms, as they still do, while in the company of other men, but not in mixed company—except perhaps by a tough, loud, and perhaps obnoxious person unfamiliar with "polite company."[23]

The term "heifers" remained popular in men's circles for a century or more. And, moreover, it was used by cowboy poets contemporary to Chittenden, including James Barton Adams in "The Cowboy's Dance Song." In another poem, "At a Cowboy Dance," Adams referred to women as "sagehens."[24]

The phrase "climb the grape vine" may refer to the idea that young men ought to take a chance and dance with one of the beautiful women who are present. In translation, the phrase relates to some Native American creation myths, especially from the Southwest. In addition, creation stories of Mandans of the Missouri River basin in North Dakota suggest that some members of the early tribe, whose homeland was a subterranean world, decided to climb a huge grape vine whose roots extended down into their country. After climbing for some time, they reached a sunny, bright world full of plants and animals. Upon returning to their underground home, their reports were encouraging enough that the entire tribe determined to take a chance and climb the grape vine.[25]

Becky Davidson explains the "jest skip her waterfall." It refers, she writes, "to a style of dress popular" in the 1880s. "The skirt was not fully hooped, but [had] boning to make it stand out much farther in the back than a dress without the additional fabric and stiff boning." Accordingly, she writes, "to get around the . . . large bustles, the men would have to skip the waterfall or swing farther out around them to do so."[26] Because of the bustles, while dancing waltzes men often danced backwards.

Fifth Stanza

The boys were tolerable skittish, the ladies powerful neat,
That old bass viol's music *just got there with both feet*!
That wailin', frisky fiddle, I never shall forget;
And Windy kept a singin'—I think I hear him yet—
"O Xes, chase your squirrels, an' cut 'em to one side,
"Spur Treadwell to the center, with Cross P Charley's bride,
"Doc. Hollis down the middle, an' twine the ladies' chain,
"Varn Andrews pen the fillies in big T Diamond's train.

"All pull yer freight tergether, neow swallow fork an' change
" 'Big Boston' lead the trail herd, through little Pitchfork's range.
"Purr round yer gentle pussies, neow rope 'em! Balance all!"
Huh! hit wuz gittin' active—"The Cowboys' Christmas Ball!"

In the fifth stanza Chittenden has Windy Bill calling several dancers by name. The "Xes," for example, refers to a cattle brand used in the 1880s by one of the big, free-range outfits in far western Jones County or in Fisher or Stonewall County. One or more cowboys from the moving cattle operation must have been present at the dance.

As a cowboy working on one of the big cow outfits, William (Will) "Spur" Treadwell became one of the early settlers of Jones County. He had moved with his mother's family from Granbury to Anson. Like many young ranch hands, Treadwell left the herding business after a few years and apprenticed as a pharmacist. Eventually, he moved to Dallas and opened a drug store.[27]

The Cross P brand belonged to one of the early ranches in Jones County. Charley P'Pool, described as the "oldest son of one of Anson's first residents," worked on the Cross P—and, thus, the name "Cross P Charley." His bride was Corrie Phipps. But, as explained by Mrs. Lucien Keene and Becky Davidson, there is more to the story: Corrie attended the 1885 ball in Anson with M. H. Rhoads, the son of the Star Hotel's owners. She met Cross P Charley at the ball "and became his bride in 1887."[28]

Dr. L. W. Hollis had moved to Anson in 1883. He served a clientele that stretched from Anson up to 150 miles distant, making house calls on horseback. He often checked his patients while they lay or sat on a kitchen table and sometimes performed surgery there. Doc Hollis, as Chittenden has Windy Bill call him, apparently was accomplished, effective, and forward looking. As Davidson writes, "According to a 1929 article in the *Abilene Reporter-News*," Hollis "performed the first appendectomy" in the Jones and Taylor counties area.[29]

The ranch poet has Windy Bill call out the names of two other men. One of them was Varn Andrews, a medical student in the mid-1880s and the son of a second local surgeon. The other was Big Boston, the nickname of Henry Foster, an Anson businessman who had arrived in Jones County from Missouri as a farmer in 1879. He was among the first county residents to try farming and to put up a barbed wire fence.[30]

Cowboys and visitors spread canvas on the ground for this 1918 dance at a Swenson-Spur Ranch camp. The dancers appear to be doing a "do-si-do" as part of a quadrille. Frank Reeves photo collection. Courtesy of Southwest Collection/Special Collections Library, Texas Tech University.

The T-Diamond Ranch, which belonged to Colonel Wash Bryant, was one of the largest cattle spreads entering Jones County in 1876. The outfit settled first along Red Mud Creek about two miles west of present Anson, site of a good, fresh-water spring. Later the T-Diamond folks moved their ranch near present Hamlin at a site close to where Fisher, Jones, and Stonewall counties meet.[31]

The "little Pitchfork's range" in Jones County should not be confused with the large Pitchfork Land and Cattle Company that still spreads across King and Dickens counties. The names and brands are similar, but the ranches are different. The pitchfork, as ranching historian David J. Murrah has indicated, "was a fairly common brand as it could be made with a single straight iron." In the Shelton and Hutto history of Jones County, the ranch in question was spelled "Pitch Fork."[32]

Also in this stanza Chittenden again has the dance caller using a term—"fillies" this time—that most men speaking in mixed company would not have used in the 1880s. Windy Bill, rather uncouth if Chittenden describes him accurately, was a loud, rough character who few people would challenge, but many liked nonetheless. Chittenden mentions him favorably in at least one other poem, a poem in which Windy Bill is an employee at the Chittenden Ranch.[33]

Sixth Stanza

The dust riz fast an' furious, we all just galloped 'round,
Till the scenery got so giddy, that Z Bar Dick was downed.
We buckled to our partners, an' told 'em to hold on,
Then shook our hoofs like lightning, until the early dawn.
Don't tell me 'bout cotillions, or germans. No sir-'ee!
That whirl at Anson City just takes the cake with me.
I'm sick of lazy shufflin's, of them I've had my fill,
Give me a frontier breakdown, backed up by Windy Bill.
McAllister ain't nowhere! when Windy leads the show,
I've seen 'em both in harness, an' so I sorter know—
Oh, Bill, I sha'n't forget yer, and I'll oftentimes recall,
That lively-gaited sworray—"The Cowboys' Christmas Ball."

In the sixth and final stanza, Chittenden has the quadrilles moving ever faster, the men holding their partners tighter. Some of the participants, such as the cowboy from the Z Bar Ranch, had consumed a bit of alcohol, thus the reference to the scenery turning giddy and Dick being "downed."

Cotillions, a polite forerunner to the fast-paced quadrilles, can be traced back to France in the eighteenth century. A cotillion, from the French word for petticoat, was a pattered social dance originally for four couples with the dance name reflecting a brief show of petticoats when women turned as they changed partners. The dance came to America about 1772 or just before the Revolutionary War. The reference to "germans" has to do with either a German version of the cotillion, which had been introduced into New York City's elite society about 1854, or a classical waltz. Although Chittenden does not mention it, a grand cotillion dance was usually a classic waltz. Our Eastern-bred author, who knew about cotillions, writes that he preferred the lively western square dances with Windy Bill shouting out the steps over the more gentle cotillions.

The McAllister reference is to Jordan Edgar McAllister, longtime manager of the LS Ranch in the Texas Panhandle. In the 1880s, McAllister started the annual Christmas balls at the ranch and usually served as the quadrille dance caller, but, if Chittenden is correct, he was not as proficient as Anson's Windy Bill. "Mister Mac," as cowboys called him, was however quite effective in handling a large cattle operation.

At the Anson Christmas ball in the Star Hotel, just as at the Frying Pan Ranch and the LS Ranch bunkhouse, the guests danced until dawn. In his poem, Chittenden describes only the quadrille and its caller William "Windy Bill" Wilkinson, but undoubtedly other dances, such as waltzes, polkas, and schottisches, were part of the dance program.

Without question Larry Chittenden's poem "The Cowboys' Christmas Ball" became popular. It was set to music early and sung by ranch hands and cowboys around their evening campfires. It was part of *Ranch Verses*, his book that went through sixteen editions before Chittenden's death in 1934. As Becky Davidson writes, Chittenden "had no idea that by writing down his poetic account of the [Star Hotel balls] of 1885" and afterward, he was leaving "a historical record," but he did of course. "By reading the verse as more than just a poem," one may rightly conclude "that the events chronicled . . . offer clues to how the citizens of [Anson and Jones County] lived and celebrated together."[34] The poem represents cultural history in West Texas as well as popular entertainment during the frontier era.

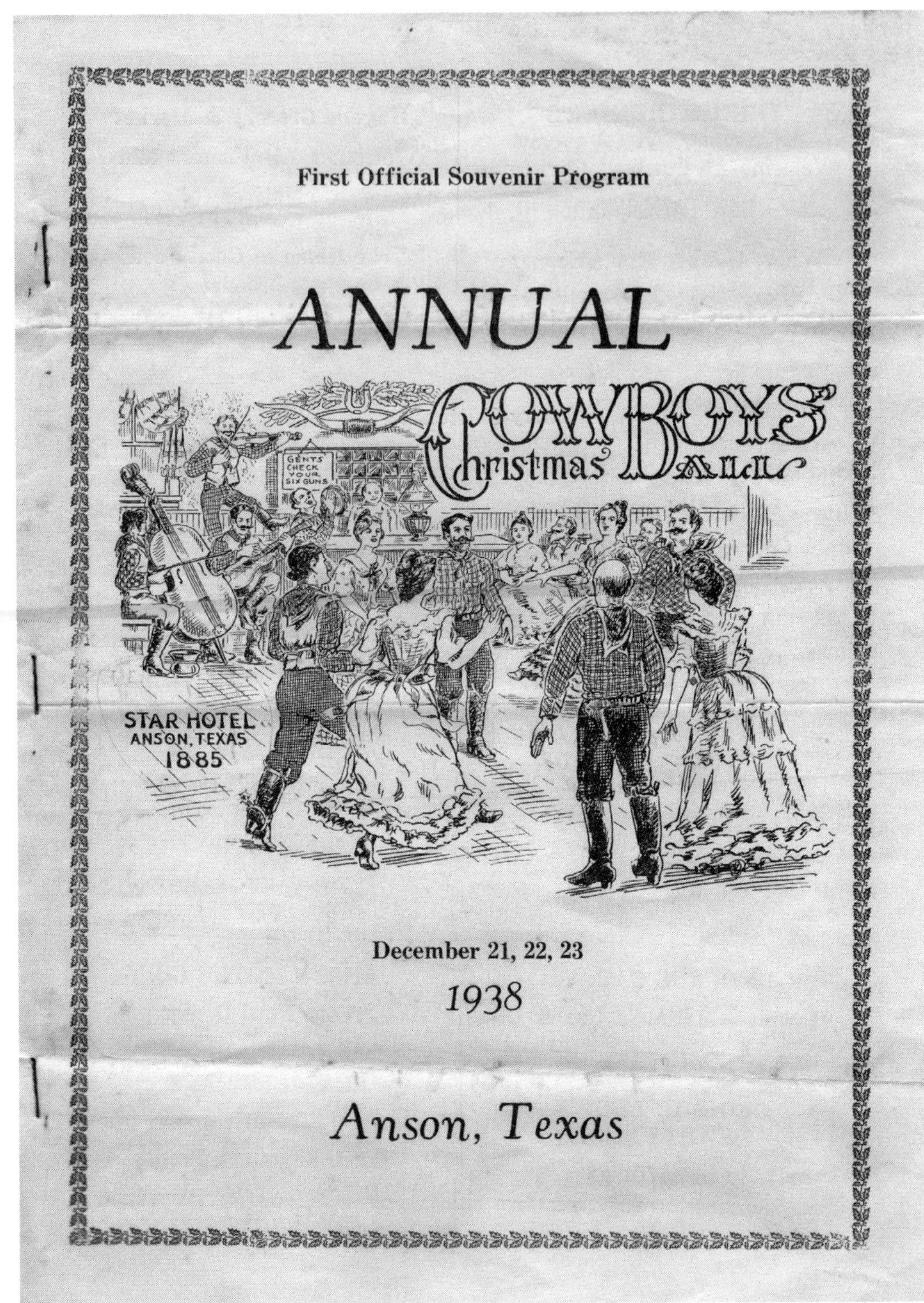
First Official Souvenir Program

ANNUAL

COWBOYS' Christmas BALL

December 21, 22, 23

1938

Anson, Texas

(Pages 72–77) Several pages from the first official program for the Texas Cowboys' Christmas Ball, 1938. Courtesy of Anson–Jones Museum.

Larry Chittenden

Again scenes which William Lawrence — (Larry) Chittenden Jones County's poet-laureate described are being lived by old-timers who inspired the famous "Cowboys Christmas Ball."

Cowboy Poet

The poet was born March 23 1862 in New Jersey and came to Texas in 1883 when he began ranch life reflected in his principal works.

ANSON SPOT CASH GROCERY

Welcome Visitors

Phone 278

FIRST NATIONAL BANK

Serving this territory nearly fifty years.

Anson, Texas

The Cowboys' Christmas Ball

—BY LARRY CHITTENDEN.—

'Way out in Western Texas, where the Clear Fork's water flow,
Where the cattle are "a-browzin'" an' the Spanish ponies grow;
Where the Northers "come a-whistlin'" from beyond the Neutral strip;
And the prairie dogs are sneezin, as if they had "The Grip";
Where the coyotes come a-howlin' 'round the ranches after dark,
And the mocking-birds are singin' to the lovely "medder lark";
Where the 'possum and the badger and rattlesnakes abound,
And the monstrous stars are winkin' o'er a wilderness profound;
Where lonesome, tawny prairies melt into airy streams,
While the Double Mountains slumber, in heavenly kinds of dreams
Where the antelope is grazin' and the lonely plovers call—
It was there that I attended "The Cowboys' Christmas Ball."

The town was Anson City old Jones' county seat,
Where they raise Polled Angus cattle, and waving whiskered wheat;
Where the air is soft and "bammy," an' dry an' full of health,
And the prairies is explodin' with agricultural wealth,
Where they print the Texas Western, that Hec McCann supplies,
With news and yarns and stories, uv most amazin' size,
Where Frank Smith "pulls the badger" on knowin' tenderfeet,
And Democracy's triumphant, and mighty hard to beat
Where lives that good old hunter John Milsap from Lamar
Who "used to be the Sheriff back East, in Paris, Sah."
'T was there, I say at Anson, with the lively "Wider Wall,"
That I went to that reception, "The Cowboys' Christmas Ball."

The boys had left the ranches and come to town in piles·
The ladies—"kinder scatterin," had gathered in for miles.
And yet the place was crowded, as I remember well,
'T was got for the occasion, at "The Morning Star Hotel."
The music was fiddle an' a lively tambourine,
And a "viol come imported," by the stage from Abilene.
The room was togged out gorgeous—with mistletoe and shawls,
And candles flickered frescoes, around the airy walls,
And "wimmin folks" looked lovely—the boys looked kinder treed,
Till their leader commenced yellin' "Whoa! fellers, let's stampede."
And the music started sighin,' an' a-wailin' through the hall,
As a kind of introduction to "The Cowboys' Christmas Ball."

(Continued Next Page.)

J. O. McKeever
Cleaner - Hatter
Phone 74

Pittman Cafe
Est. 1901
Mr. and Mrs.
Al Williams

Compliments
BARNES DRUG
Anson

BILL'S CAFE
Largest
Hamburgers In
The World

Visitors . . .
You're Invited to
Holmes Coffee Shop

THE HUB

The Store Without Competition

Phone 52

Gray's

Service Station

Phone 205

Hi-School Cafe

Good Sandwiches
Coffee

Opposite Hi School

Compliments

Jones County Abstract Company

Lee McCaleb
J. W. Purifoy

Anson

Dunwody . . .

The Tailor

Phone . . 300

THE COWBOYS CHRISTMAS BALL COMMITTEES EXTEND TO EVERY VISITOR A HEARTY WELCOME TO ANSON

Compliments

R. B. Spencer

& Company

Compliments

Mayfield Beauty Shop

ANSON AUTO PARTS

Phone . . . 35

Welcome to . . .

Wilson Grocery & Market

Staple - Fancy Groceries

Phone 132

HUDSON IMPLEMENT CO.

WELCOMES YOU

Season's Greetings to . . .

The Cowboys Christmas Ball

HOME FURNITURE CO.

Anson, Texas

Panhandle Abstract Company

Established 1886

Anson, Texas Phone 243

The leader was a feller that came from Swenson's Ranch,
They called him "Windy Billy," from "little Deadman's Branch."
His rig was "kinder keerless," big spurs and high-heeled boots;
He had the reputation that comes when "fellers shoots,"
His voice was like a bugle upon the mountain's height;
His feet were animated, an' A MIGHTY MOVIN' SIGHT
When he commenced to holler "Neow fellers, stake yer pen!
"Lock horns ter all them heifers, an' russel 'em like men.
"Salcot yer lovely critter' neow swing an' let 'em go,
"Climb the grape vine 'round 'em—all hands do-ce-do!
"You Mavericks, jine the round-up—jest skip her waterfall,"
Huh! hit was gettin' happy "The Cowboys' Christmas Ball!"

The boys were tolerable skittish, the ladies powerful neat,
That old bass viol's music JUST GOT THERE WITH BOTH FEET!
That wailin,' frisky fiddle, I never shall forget;
And Windy kept a-singin'—I think I hear him yet—
"O Yes, chase your squirrels, an' cut 'em to one side,
"Spur Treadwell to the center with Cross P Charley's bride,
"Doc. Hollis down the middle, an' twine the ladies chain,
"Varn Andrews pen the fillies in big T Diamond's train.
"All pull yer freight together neow, swallow fork an' change,
"'Big Boston' lead the trail herd, through little Pitchfork's range.
"Purr 'round yer gentle pussies, neow rope 'em! Balance all!"
Huh! hit wuz gettin' active—"The Cowboys' Christmas Ball."

The dust riz fast an' furious, we all just galloped 'round,
Till the scenery got so giddy, that Z Bar Dick was downed.
We buckled on our partners, an' tole 'em to hold on,
Then shook our hoofs like lightening, until the early dawn.
Don't tell me 'bout cotillions, or germans. No sir'ee!
That whirl at Anson City just takes the cake with me.
I'm sick of lazy shufflin's, of them I've had my fill,
Give me a frontier break-down, backed up by Windy Bill.
McAllister ain't nowhar! when Windy leads the show
I've seen 'em both in harness, and so I sorter know—
Oh, Bill, I shan't forget yer, and I'll oftentimes recall,
That lively gaited sworray—"The Cowboys' Christmas Ball."

Geo. Pearce

Boot and

Shoe

Shop

"Boots Made To Measure"

Our Compliments

Bluebird Beauty

Shoppe

Clyde's Wrecking

Shop

Welcomes You

Compliments of . . .

MAYFIELD & GLEASON

Grocery and Market

JOHN NEVILLE

Boot, Shoe, Harness and Saddle

Shop

East Side Square Anson

That Lively Gaited Sworray—

"THE COWBOYS' CHRISTMAS BALL"

WE ALL JUST GALLOPED 'ROUND...
Some of the dresses were in keeping with the dance steps of yesterday, but that did not keep the dancers from having a good time. This picture shows a group doing the *Virginia Reel*.

THAT WAILIN', FRISKY FIDDLE . . .
C. L. Wright of Anson played a few tunes on his fiddle at the 1937 ball, just as he did in 1885.

HUH! HIT WAS GETTIN' HAPPY . . . .
Hundreds of couples are shown dancing the *Heel and Toe Polka*. Some of the younger generation were a little self-conscious as they endeavored to keep pace with their elders as they did the old time dances.

THE "WIMMIN FOLKS" LOOKED LOVELY . . . .
Mrs. Hattie Moran of Anson and Mrs. Mary L. Roberts of Paducah. Each admits 71. They attended the 1937 ball and were present at the original ball in 1885.

HIS FEET WERE ANIMATED, AN' A MIGHTY, MOVIN' SIGHT . . . .
The caller had just bellowed *"Right and Left All"* when this picture was taken. The caller and one of the dancers was Judge Chas. E. Coombes of Stamford, who can shake a "wicked hoof" as [illegible]ll as give an iron-clad legal opinion.

CHAPTER FIVE

Cowboy Poetry and Pioneer Dances

In the 1880s, when Larry Chittenden wrote "The Cowboys' Christmas Ball," folk poetry and rural, agrarian music fell easily into traditional dance and muse forms that were popular on the westward-moving Texas frontier. Oral, or folk, poetry at the time tended to be quite simple. It often rhymed, used an iambic meter, and in West Texas cattle country utilized vernacular dialect common on Western ranges. At pioneer dances, the musical instrumentation was simple. Fiddles and banjos, perhaps a Jew's harp (juice harp, gewgaw, guimbarde, or "cowboy mouth harp"), and often a harmonica or "mouth organ" could be found.

Put another way, in the late nineteenth-century Southwest, including Texas, cowboy poetry became popular, pioneer dances attracted attention, and music accompanying the dances remained traditional. Musical instruments represented items that could be transported along the western edge of settlement, or they were homemade. Older, familiar Christian church hymns, such as Amazing Grace and Rock of Ages, secular dance tunes, such as The Arkansas Traveler, and dances, such as the Virginia reel or any number of waltzes, dominated the music. But cowboy poetry and song, writes David Stanley, were often "interchangeable because poems were frequently set to music, [usually] to traditional tunes or popular music of the day."[1]

With publication of his celebrated book *Ranch Verses* in 1893, Larry Chittenden became the first commercially successful cowboy poet. Cattle trail cowboys from at least 1866—soon after the Civil War when long, overland trail drives began in earnest—had been constructing verses and reciting poetry (think "The Old Chisholm Trail" with its countless verses) around campfires and singing quiet ballads as they night-herded their two-year-old steers and young cows toward Sedalia, Missouri, or in the 1870s to rail heads in Kansas or beyond to the northern Great Plains. Also, Frank Desprez, a London theater critic who enjoyed only a brief time in the West, published in 1882 a poem, "Lasca," in the Montana *Stock Growers' Journal.* According to founding director of the National Cowboy Poetry Gathering in Elko, Nevada, Hal Cannon, it "was widely recited by cowboys" and eventually became "a popular performance piece in Chautauqua presentations all over" the country.[2]

A few years later in 1886, Lysius "Parson" Gough (1862–1940), a Texas cowboy and schoolteacher, published *Western Travels and Other Rhymes*, perhaps the first serious collection of cowboy verse. Gough released the book while he was principal of Pilot Point Institute in Denton County. He later settled in the Texas Panhandle, where he studied law, taught school, raised huge amounts of wheat, served as the first judge of Castro County and from 1923 to 1928 as president of the Texas Wheat Growers Association, and wrote additional poetry, including *Spur Jingles and Saddle Songs* (1935).[3]

But, Chittenden, who had written poetry for a dozen years and had published poems in newspapers and magazines in New York, Texas, and elsewhere, produced the first highly popular book of western cowboy poetry. The book was a huge success and went through many printings and later several revisions and enlargements.[4] Like Gough's work, it may have stimulated additional folk poetry and encouraged cowboy poets to send their poems to newspapers and magazines.

As Chittenden's book gained attention, other western poets, including Nathan Howard "Jack" Thorp, were collecting cowboy songs. Thorp, like Chittenden, was from a wealthy New York City family. Although Harvard educated, he became a cowboy in New Mexico in the 1890s. There, upon hearing a black cowboy singing a sad cowboy song, Thorp tried his hand at poetry. Not long afterward, while trailing a herd of cattle from New Mexico to Texas, he wrote "Little Joe the Wrangler," and at the same time, 1898, began collecting cowboy poems and songs. In 1908, he published twenty-three of them, as well as his own poem "Little Joe," in *Songs of the Cowboys.*[5]

Thorp's little book inspired others, particularly Harvard-based musicologist John A. Lomax, to collect cowboy songs and poetry. Unfortunately, as Lomax has demonstrated, names of many of the poems' authors are unknown or forgotten. Even some authors of the period's very best cowboy poetry remained anonymous.[6] Still, before the turn of the century self-published books and small pamphlets of cowboy poetry had appeared, and several folk poets had become widely recognized for their work through publication of poems in newspapers, magazines, and livestock journals.

Among them was James Barton Adams (1843–1918). Like Gough and Chittenden, he was among the few western poets to turn out a book of cowboy poetry before 1900. He was a Civil War veteran who became a newspaper man in Denver, Colorado. He worked on the *Denver Post*, the *Denver Times*, and the *Rocky Mountain News*, and saw some of his poems printed in these newspapers where hundreds of people read them. In 1889, Adams published a book of poetry, *Breezy Western Verse*. Later, John A. Lomax included some of his poems, as well as several of Thorp's pieces, in *Songs of the Cattle Trail and Cow Camp*.[7]

Another poet who published his work prior to 1900 was Robert V. Carr (1877–1931). Carr wanted to be a cowboy and sought jobs on the ranches of South Dakota, where, he says, he mainly bothered the cooks and wrote poetry. Eventually, he became a newspaper man, working on or editing several papers in western South Dakota and later at the *Denver Times*. He wrote poetry and short fiction, some of which was published in western magazines. In 1902, he published a collection of poems titled *Black Hills Ballads*, and in 1912, he came out with *Cowboy Lyrics*. Like Adams and Chittenden, some of his poems appeared in Lomax's *Songs of the Cattle Trail and Cow Camp*.[8]

Chittenden, Adams, and Carr, if not superior poets, at least remained popular. They were, writes Hal Cannon, among a group of authors who "wrote a good deal of poetry for the popular market and it shows in their subjects and style."[9] Most of the others in Cannon's group wrote in the 1910s. They included such self-published authors as Carmen William "Curley" Fletcher (1892–1954), Gail Gardner (1892–1988), and Bruce Kiskaddon (1878–1950). Fletcher's "The Strawberry Roan," a selection in his 1917 poetry pamphlet, has become one of the most popular of all cowboy poems. Gardner's 1917 poem "Sierry Petes" ("Tying Knots in the Devil's Tail") is easily sung and was often pirated. Kiskaddon, remembered for his skill at describing cowboy life as it existed in the Old West, has been called the most influential of all cowboy poets.[10]

A third part of Cannon's early group of favorite cowboy poets included several who published with mainstream presses in New York or elsewhere.

The clique included Charles Badger Clark, Jr. (1883–1957), E. A. "Earl" Brininstool (1870–1957), Arthur Chapman (1873–1935), Elliott C. Lincoln (1884–1970), Henry Herbert Knibbs (1875–1945), and S. Omar Barker (1894–1985). According to some scholars, Knibbs, an easterner, and Barker from New Mexico, display perhaps a bit more knowledge of cows, horses, and cowboy ways—at least from a cowboy's perspective—than the other poets. Moreover, Barker, writes Cannon, saw himself as a professional writer—"I'm a western poet, not a cowboy poet"—and wanted to set himself apart from the "folk versifiers."[11]

From 1905 to 1935, Cannon's group of twelve poets helped create something like a cowboy poetry golden age. They wrote books of poetry. Their poetry also appeared in newspapers and magazines, on calendars, in livestock journals, and elsewhere. They were widely read and copied, and especially in the case of Gardner, others claimed the poetry as their own. In a few places, such as each new edition of John Lomax's *Songs of the Cattle Trail and Cow Camp* and Walter Prescott Webb's 1931 *The Great Plains* or in Harvard University classes on the literary history of America, their poetry received serious scholarly attention. Their work during the golden age represented important aspects of earlier folk traditions.

The golden age of which they were a part took its inspiration from several sources. One source may have been the "fabricated" cowboy hero William "Buck" Taylor in Buffalo Bill's Wild West and Congress of Rough Riders, a hero also immortalized in Prentiss Ingraham's 1887 dime novel *Buck Taylor, King of the Cowboys.* Western heroes in later print fiction, such as the principal character in Owen Wister's 1902 ground-breaking novel *The Virginian* or maybe the heroes of Zane Grey's early westerns, represent other sources. Perhaps early western films—the silent ones—inspired them. Or, maybe, as in the case of Bruce Kiskaddon, who has been called the cowboy poet laureate of America, they saw an older cowboy way of life disappearing and wanted little more than to memorialize western cattle-raising and the open range activities associated with it.[12]

Whatever the case, cowboy poetry slipped from popularity in the late 1930s and during World War II. It appeared less often in newspapers, magazines, and livestock journals, except perhaps for Kiskaddon's work. In fact, Kiskaddon's poetry continued to appear in livestock journals long after his death in 1950. Nonetheless, at mid-century, cowboy poetry was in decline—or so it seemed.

Several couples dancing at the Texas Cowboys' Christmas Ball, c. 1940s or early 1950s. Courtesy of Texas Cowboys' Christmas Ball Association.

Cowboy poetry had not disappeared, but clearly it had changed and evolved. In Larry Chittenden's days, rhymed and metered verse, a structure that facilitated memorization, characterized it. In form and style, it can be traced from Texas and the greater West back through the Old South and colonial Virginia to England, particularly southeastern England. The style was a common, oral form that ballad singers had used for centuries, and perhaps accounts for Chittenden's *Ranch Verses* enjoying enormous popularity in the South and in England.[13]

Chittenden's famous "The Cowboys' Christmas Ball" is typical of such popular folk poetry. It rhymed in a common aa bb pattern. It had a regular meter, in this case a lyrical one, easily put to music. Its content contrasted East and West to the detriment of the East. It described a familiar cowboy event, but in this one with men and women together in town rather than a lonely cowboy at work on an empty prairie.[14]

In general, cowboy poetry in Chittenden's day, the late nineteenth and early twentieth centuries, was often either a description of the harsh realities of working the range or a romanticized version of the cowboy way of life. Sometimes it was spontaneous, created around the campfire or on horseback while watching cattle or riding a fence line. More often the composer worked hard on his creation, checking the meter, considering the rhyme scheme, and perfecting its message. It might contain moral lessons; tell of future plans, a lost love, or the death of a friend; poke fun at "the boss," a haughty colleague, or a high-born tenderfoot; describe an ornery cow, a favorite horse, or the life of an unusual character.

The best cowboy poetry of the period, even the nostalgic, lonely pieces, was folk poetry, a ballad easy to listen to. And, by definition, cowboy poetry, traditional or modern, must tell a good story. Chittenden's "The Cowboys' Christmas Ball" is such a poem, that is, a ballad that tells a story in a lively fashion.

Likewise, Chittenden's first book of poems, *Ranch Verses,* is also characteristic of folk poetry—in this case the western cattle frontier. Chittenden composed most of the 133 poems on the Chittenden Ranch near Anson, Texas, but they are not all ranch verses. There are poems of the seacoast, of his Montclair, New Jersey, birthplace, and of New York City. Many of the poems are about young women ("The Western Girl," "The Southern Girl," and "The California Girl," among others). Some poems teach lessons, moral and otherwise, describe the weather, or touch on philosophy ("What Is Life?"), but the collection, in Hal Cannon's words, is "rife with Victorian stuffiness and sentimentality."[15] The nearly thirty poems in the book related to livestock ranch and range activities romanticize cowboys and their late nineteenth-century lifeways.

One hundred years later, cowboy poetry was different. After the days of trail-drive poetry, it had evolved and changed. In other words, the poetry of Larry Chittenden, Frank Desprez, James Barton Adams, and such other early cowboy poets as Badger Clark and Bruce Kiskaddon gave way in the second half of the twentieth century to less structured forms, and sometimes it contained irregular rhymes and broken meter. Eventually, it included free verse.

Also in the late twentieth century, cowboy poetry enjoyed a renaissance. Having moved through a golden age at the beginning of the century and a period of decline afterward, it regained its luster and again found a niche. Since the mid-1980s, there has been a renewed interest in cowboy poetry as folk art and oral literature.[16]

In 2013, many scholars still see cowboy poetry as a folk tradition. They see it as light, popular verse with little craft and less substance. Others, however, see its modern popularity as part of a larger avant garde movement.

To them, cowboy poetry is to the rural South and West what rap poetry is to the urban North and East: orality is its core. As Nancy Mclelland writes, contemporary cowboy poetry might be "interesting" on the printed page, but it "cries out for recitation."[17]

The cowboy poetry renaissance and the continuing popularity of oral folk performances led in part to the success of modern cowboy poetry gatherings. The gatherings, in turn, have increased cowboy poetry's popularity.

Modern cowboy poetry gatherings began in 1985. Hal Cannon, who lived in Idaho at the time, initiated the event, but several others were involved in its organization, including Jim Griffith, director of Tucson's Southwest Folklore Center, and such western folklorists and poets as Waddie Mitchell. They chose Elko, Nevada, as the site for their gathering because it was in the middle of ranch country and, although a small town, it held requisite facilities to host the event.[18]

The Elko Cowboy Poetry Gathering attracted about one hundred people in 1985. Most of them were folk poets, many of whom lived in the vicinity of Elko. Because everyone in attendance judged the event a success, its leaders repeated the poetry gathering in 1986. Indeed, it has been held each year since the inaugural staging, and in some years nearly eight thousand people attended.[19]

The Elko gathering, coupled with the rising popularity of cowboy poetry, led to similar poetry events. In 2010, as David Stanley, a folklorist at Westminster College in Salt Lake City, has written, perhaps "150 regional, state, and local gatherings" occurred.[20] Many of them were comprised of more than poetry. Some of the larger ones, such as at Elko, Nevada, include music, historic presentations, films, panel discussions, and other activities. Barbeques and chuck wagon breakfasts are common at the gatherings, and western art and craft exhibits can be viewed. In general, attendees gather to eat, drink, swap stories, and learn about western cowboy culture.

In Texas, the oldest and one of the most successful gatherings is the Alpine event, usually staged in February at Sul Ross State University. Like the Elko gathering, it includes music, historical presentations, and barbeques in addition to the poetry. In Lubbock, cowboy poetry is an important part of the annual National Cowboy Symposium and Celebration, which like Elko and Alpine includes western arts and crafts, chuck wagon breakfasts, and related events.

Anson, Texas, home of the Texas Cowboys' Christmas Ball, hosts a cowboy poetry gathering. Taking full advantage of the popular Christmas ball,

Michael Martin Murphey outside Pioneer Hall, c. 2000. Photo by Jimmy Boyd. Courtesy of Michael Martin Murphey.

the poetry event organizers call it the "Larry Chittenden Memorial Cowboy Celebration." This event began in 1992 and takes place over a two-day period during the same weekend as the cowboy Christmas ball. The venue is the two-story Anson Opera House, built in 1907 and located on the north side of the courthouse square. In 1997, the organizers added a western art exhibit and a "Bits, Spurs and Trappings Show." Held on Friday and Saturday afternoons, its leaders hoped that people attending the Christmas ball every evening would visit the cowboy poetry presentations in the afternoon.[21]

Whether recited at modern poetry gatherings, around an evening campfire, or along an old nineteenth-century cattle trail, cowboy poetry has a deep background. Because of its history and storytelling, balladic form, cowboy poetry in the American West has lent itself to singing and dance. Cowboys sang their verses to cows and colleagues alike, sometimes composing short verses on the run, including scores of verses to "The Old Chisholm Trail," a genuine cowboy song and perhaps the most universally sung western folk poem.[22]

Another genuine cowboy song, as noted above, is Jack Thorp's "Little Joe the Wrangler." As with Gail Gardner's "Sierry Petes," several individuals and groups pirated the song, including John Lomax. Composed during an

1898 cattle drive from Chimney Lake, New Mexico, to Higgins in Lipscomb County, Texas, it became one of the most famous cowboy songs of the early twentieth century. Believing "Little Joe" was a traditional old favorite, music companies distributed many recordings of the popular song, but Thorp, despite legal proceedings to protect his copyrighted verse, was unable to collect royalties.

The popular old trail song is typical of how many cowboy poems became part of western music. In a catchy meter, the poems told an often-familiar western story in rhyme, one easily memorized, easily set to music, and easily copied or pirated. As noted earlier, just a few years after it appeared in print, cowboys in New Mexico were singing Chittenden's "The Cowboys' Christmas Ball," and others not only soon and easily set Gail Gardner's "Sierry Petes" to music but also claimed that they wrote the popular work.

The process was not difficult. Joseph G. McCoy, one of the original promoters of the western cattle trade, wrote, "Singing hymns to Texan steers is the peculiar forte of a genuine cowboy. . . . And it is surprising how quiet the herd will be so long as they can hear the human voice." According to Will James, author of *Cow Country*, "When the last meal of the day was over and as the big herd was gathered close together and grazed to the bed-grounds for the night, the old songs of the cow-camps and trail-herd were brought to life."[23] Much of the singing was without musical accompaniment.

Nonetheless, around a campfire, someone might bring out a harmonica ("mouth-organ" as poet Badger Clark called it). At the ranch bunkhouse, one might find a guitar, but fiddles and banjos were the most common instruments on the cattle frontier. Jew's harps ("mouth-harp") and once in a while an accordion could be found among the cowboys.

In town or at the home of a successful rancher, there might be larger musical instruments. In a ranch home, one might find a small piano, and in a larger frontier community, especially in a larger railroad town such as Abilene, one might find an organ.[24] In 1885 at the Star Hotel in Anson, a very young town at the time, someone played a tambourine at the Christmastime dance and a bass viol came with its owner—probably—on the stagecoach from Abilene. In addition, there was a fiddle or two, and at subsequent dances someone might have brought a banjo or maybe even a guitar to the cowboy ball.[25]

Sometimes the dances were rollicking. Joseph G. McCoy described a cowboy dance in an Abilene, Kansas, dance hall. Cowboys, having just finished a long cattle drive from Texas, stepped onto the dance floor still wearing their hats, spurs, and revolvers. A cowboy, having drunk too much liquor, McCoy writes, "plunges in and 'hoes it down' at a terrible rate in the most approved yet awkward country style, often swinging his partner clear off of the floor for an entire circle, then 'balance all,' with an occasional demoniacal yell."[26] There were, in addition, "stag dances," that is, "a dance without women," as Guy Logsdon writes, "where cowboys drank, danced, and raised hell" and recited poems of "gross obscenity."[27]

More characteristic cowboy dances were polite events. Men, women, and children, all dressed in their finest clothes, arrived by wagon, buggy, or horseback. Some of them came from great distances to attend the dance. Men outnumbered women at such events, and as a result women found little time to rest. They were on the dance floor constantly and in one night of dancing might wear through the soles of their shoes.

Because fewer women than men attended such pioneer dances, often some men agreed to take the female part for the quadrilles. Indeed, as Vanita Parrett writes, "some men unselfishly tied handkerchiefs on their arms and, thus 'heifer-branded,' danced 'lady fashion'" even for waltzes and polkas.[28] A fiddle player most often provided the music, but on occasion someone might have an accordion. As noted, Larry Chittenden indicates that at the Cowboys' Christmas Ball in Anson, Texas, in 1885, there was a fiddle player plus a tambourine and a bass viol, clearly an unusual number of instruments for a pioneer dance.

In the early days of pioneer dances, quadrilles, or square dance patterns, were common. Such dances were part of the folk tradition brought to America from Ireland and Scotland and spread into the southern Appalachian Mountains. From there the tradition, derived from jigs (6/8 time) and reels (2/4 time), moved westward with pioneers into Texas along the expanding cattle-raising frontier. Nineteenth-century dance steps and patterns were, unlike modern square dances, common, traditional, and easy to learn through experience. And, as noted, a fiddle often served as the lead instrument.

Quadrilles needed a "caller" to direct the dance. Usually a male, the caller required a strong voice and a carefree manner. The calls reflected oral traditions and common usage, but over time took on fresh interpretations. The caller, according to folklorist J. R. Craddock, "chanted the calls in a rhythmic monotone that fitted well with the music of the fiddle . . . , sometimes calling from memory, filling in forgotten parts with new words, and often inventing entirely new calls."[29]

William "Windy Bill" Wilkinson of Larry Chittenden's "The Cowboys'

Christmas Ball" was a typical square dance caller. He was a self-confident, easygoing, and solid cowhand who worked on several different ranches in the Jones County area. Loud-mouthed and talkative, he knew the dance calls and possessed a voice that could be heard from a long ways off.[30]

The calls were common and easy to pick up. As explained by Vanita Parrett, the quadrille with four couples usually opened with an introductory move ("figure") and call:

All join hands and circle left.
Honors right and honors left. ("Honors" were bows.)

In this "figure each man bowed first to his partner, on his right, and then his 'corner,' on his left." Women return the bow. As the dance progressed, there were plenty of rhyming lines in the calls, which made the dance moves easier to follow. For example:

Now you're right and now you're wrong,
Now your right and you can't go wrong.

Sometimes the first line was superfluous, the second line giving the call:

Chicken on a hillside picking up gravel;
Meet your partner and everybody travel.

Or:

Chew your tobacco and spit your snuff,
Swing your partner and strut your stuff.[31]

While they were by far the most popular, quadrilles were not the only folk dances at a pioneer ball. Waltzes, polkas, reels, gallops, schottisches, and other dances were interspersed with the square dances. Over time, new dances appeared and older dances took on different forms. The modern western square dance, for example, is different from and far more complex than the quadrilles of Chittenden's day.

In the twentieth century, as square dancing became more complex, waltzes and schottisches gained greater acceptance. During the first half of the century, the Cotton-Eyed Joe, adopted from polka rhythms, became a popular folk song and dance. A modified line dance and fiddle-based song, the Cotton-Eyed Joe predates the Civil War. Slaves sung its lyrics. In 1882, one of the poem's many variants was published. About early mid-century the dance may have gone into a brief decline, but after the 1960s an Al Dean version of the song became one of the most played records in Texas jukebox history. And, the dance, after the 1980 release of the movie *Urban Cowboy*, again enjoyed a craze in the West. It became for a time, writes Betty Casey, the "South Texas National Anthem."[32]

At modern country music balls, according to Betty Casey, the shuffle step, which "has been erroneously called the 'Texas two-step'" remains "the most popular dance step for couples on Texas dance floors." The dance in its most popular form (4/4 time) is a round dance in which the partners in close formation moved counter-clockwise around the floor. Like the Cotton-Eyed Joe and modern waltzes, the dance has many variants.[33]

Just as folk songs and pioneer-style dance favorites have changed over time, instrumentation has likewise evolved. Guitars became a favorite instrument. Small dance bands appeared, and by the mid-twentieth century, drums, adopted from large orchestras and swing music of the 1930s and 1940s, had become an important part of honky-tonk dance band music. By the mid-1950s, some of the energetic, high-voltage, drum-and-guitar sounds that dominated rock and roll music had made their way into country music. Keyboards, developed from piano music, and steel guitars also became necessary parts of a country music dance band.

Through all such changes and innovations, the fiddle remained important at western-style dances. Indeed, as late as 1984 the song "If You're Gonna Play in Texas (You Gotta Have a Fiddle in the Band)" reached number-one ranking on the *Billboard* Hot Country Singles chart. Murray Kellum and Dan Mitchell wrote the now-classic tune, and the American country music band Alabama recorded it. The song reinforces the importance of fiddle music.

At the modern Texas Cowboys' Christmas Ball in Anson, fiddles have been present from the beginning. The house bands, including the Drug Store Cowboys and Abe Crutchfield in the early years, Lariat for a few years, and Muddy Creek beginning in 2008, have fiddle players. Michael Martin Murphey, who has played at the Christmas ball since 1993 and appreciates the ball's long history, has fiddle players in his Rio Grande band.[34]

In the end, although much has changed in country music dances, much remains the same. Fiddles are still common. Murphey still uses a harmonica for such tunes as "Red River Valley." Various waltzes, schottisches, and polkas remain popular. At the Texas Cowboys' Christmas Ball, the Virginia reel, the varsovienne (varsouviana) or "Put Your Little Foot," which can be danced as a waltz, schottische, polka, or a mazurka variant, and "The Eyes of Texas" for the grand march are constants.[35]

Cowboy poetry, although considerably different from the Victorian simplicity of Larry Chittenden, continues to be popular. It no longer appears much in newspapers and magazines, but, as Dana Gioia, Hal Cannon, Guy Logsdon, and others have noted, poetry books and journals are abundant, and scholarly books that tackle issues related to oral folk traditions and cowboy poetry appear from publishers on a regular basis. Moreover, it is a subject for serious discussion in university classrooms—even in honors classes—as Andy Wilkinson, adjunct professor of music and composition at Texas Tech University, has explained.

Folk poetry was not an issue at the 1880s cowboy dances in Anson, Texas, but dance traditions and folk music were. Participants in the ball at M. G. Rhoads' Star Hotel understood basic quadrille (square dance) steps and movements; they knew common waltz and polka steps; and they enjoyed the simple music that the fiddles, tambourine, and bass viol provided. Most participants, some of whom had come from many miles away, danced all night before heading home in the early morning in the wagon or buggy that had brought them.

Modern country music dances are different. They may extend well past midnight, but the instrumentation is more sophisticated, the dance halls are larger, and square dancing is seldom present. The dress of the dancers is different as well. In the 1880s, during waltzes and a few other dances at the Star Hotel, for example, to avoid the bustle that stood out behind women's dresses, men often danced backward. In 2013, the cumbersome dress style is out of favor at western dances and women almost always dance backward, often in boots or high-heeled shoes.

The folk poetry of Larry Chittenden in the late 1880s inspired the modern Texas Cowboys' Christmas Ball. And, although the favorite dance, the quadrille, at the pioneer event has changed, as had the instrumentation, some things remain the same. As they did nearly 130 years ago, cowboys at the December dance in Anson still polish their boots, still check their hats at the door, and still leave their spurs at home. And women still wear long dresses on the dance floor of Pioneer Hall.

CHAPTER SIX

Michael Martin Murphey and the Modern Texas Cowboys' Christmas Ball

Michael Martin Murphey, the Country Music Association award–winning musician and member of the Western Music Hall of Fame, seems like a natural to headline the Texas Cowboys' Christmas Ball reenactment and celebration. Murphey, or "Murph" to his friends, is a rancher, horseman, writer and composer, singer of western songs, and a cowboy. He dresses for the part with hat, boots, vest, and bandana. He has played the historic Christmas ball for nearly twenty years and almost single-handedly spread the event's fame far beyond the Anson and Jones County areas. He has made the dance more popular than ever. In part because of his efforts, the big, colorful, family-oriented Christmas dance annually attracts people from as far away as Minnesota and Florida, California and New York, Canada, Europe, and elsewhere.

Because of Murphey's efforts the Christmas dance in Anson is no isolated phenomenon. In 1985, Murphey, who had read Larry Chittenden's unforgettable poem "The Cowboys' Christmas Ball" and for years had heard it sung, recorded his version of the song—although not released until 1987. It is a long poem, full of colorful 1880s vignettes. Because "the original words contain so many rich descriptions of frontier life in Texas," Murphey writes, he had difficulty editing the poem to fit modern demands of radio's need for a three-minute song.[1]

But, Murphey succeeded. The recording was a hit, and it started him "down the road toward reviving [the Chittenden Christmas] tradition as a tour."[2]

Leonora Barrett in foreground at the 1938 "reenactment" of the 1880s Anson Christmas dances. Frank Reeves photo collection. Courtesy of Southwest Collection/Special Collections Library, Texas Tech University.

Murphey began his annual Christmas tour in Amarillo, Texas. The first year, 1986, he assembled an all-star cast to perform with him. The "featured artists," he writes, included "Don Edwards, Waddie Mitchell, Ian Tyson, and Chris Ledoux—all artists who shared [his] passion for cowboy music and poetry."[3]

The success in Amarillo encouraged Murphey to expand the Christmas tour. He recognized that many people in America enjoyed and even yearned for the annual revival of old western traditions with its simple folk dances and familiar frontier cowboy songs. The tour grew yearly and spread to New Mexico, Colorado, Oklahoma, and elsewhere.

Over time, Murphey experimented with an annual Cowboy Christmas Concert. By 2003, in some cities, he had adopted a theater-like performance that resembled a one-man play. As described by Nola McKey, who has written about one of the performances, after several songs, the musical presentation had Murphey "sitting by a campfire telling stories and singing songs backed by a full band." During the performance, she notes, he "weaves a comparison of 19th-century rural values and 21st-century mainstream values into his [show], using the Cowboys' Christmas Ball event as a surviving example of 'the good old days.' "[4]

In the meantime, the tour's initial success inspired a related development. In 1990, Murphey recorded *Cowboy Songs*, an album of classic cowboy tunes. It included such familiar pieces as "Tumbling Tumbleweeds," "The Old Chisholm Trail," "The Streets of Laredo" (or "Cowboy's Lament"), and Roy Rogers' "Happy Trails," among several others songs. The album sold well, achieving "gold" status, and received widespread critical acclaim from country music and folk music critics.[5]

A year later, Murphey recorded another album. Even while he expanded his tour of cowboy Christmas shows, he produced a Christmas album, *Cowboy Christmas: Cowboy Songs II*, which contains both original and traditional Christmas songs, and his version of Chittenden's Christmas poem. The same year he came out with another album, one titled *Rhymes of the Renegades: Cowboy Songs III.* A second Christmas album, *Acoustic Christmas Carols*, appeared in 1999, and four years later he released *Cowboy Christmas III.*

The success of Murphey's cowboy songs and his Christmas albums helped to promote the Christmas tour. In the early 1990s, Murphey was playing up to ten such events each year in the few weeks before Christmas. The concerts and the albums gave proof that the larger cowboy Christmas ball tradition was popular, and "very much alive and thriving."[6]

Then, in 1993, Murphey began playing the Texas Cowboys' Christmas Ball in Anson. The performance there represented a key stop in his annual tour. Like Murphey, the Texas Cowboys' Christmas Ball Association sought to keep "the flame of an important American tradition alive."[7] Both want to preserve the heritage, values, and traditional features of the Old West's range-cattle industry.

The two, Murphey and the Association, also benefitted from an unexpected but related development. The financial success of such popular period westerns as *Tombstone* (1993) helped them. Victorian-age images and costumes from *Tombstone*, which was set in the 1880s, inspired, at least temporarily, further interest in western traditions, lifeways, styles, clothing, and music. A revival, if perhaps only temporary, of western films and television shows in 2012 and 2013 may add to the interest.

In any case, as a result of the post-*Tombstone* interest, Murphey's plan for preserving America's western ranching heritage expanded. He continued to release albums of cowboy songs, moved into bluegrass, and added venue sites

Grand march at the 1938 Anson Cowboys' Christmas dance. Frank Reeves photo collection. Courtesy of Southwest Collection/Special Collections Library, Texas Tech University.

to his Cowboy Christmas Concert series. By 2012, he had played at least five hundred cowboy Christmas shows and dances. Over a short six-week period in 2013, he performed either his Christmas concert or played a Christmas dance at places from Steelville, Missouri, and Benton, Kansas, to New Mexico, and through Oklahoma and Texas all the way to the Gulf Coast.[8]

Murphey performed at some major venues. Among many other sites during his tour, Murphey and his Rio Grande band played in the Performing Arts Center at Texas A & M University-Corpus Christi, the National Cowboy and Western Heritage Museum in Oklahoma City, and the spectacular Bass Performance Hall in Fort Worth. And, of course, on the weekend before Christmas that year, Murphey was in the little town of Anson, where he played on December 21 for the twentieth time at the seventy-ninth consecutive Texas Cowboys' Christmas Ball.

The older, unique, and very special Anson event, partly by happenstance and partly by careful design, became a part of Murphey's larger Cowboy

Lively dancing in Anson high school gymnasium in 1938. Note the large number of people sitting in the gym bleachers, watching or waiting to dance. Frank Reeves photo collection. Courtesy of Southwest Collection/Special Collections Library, Texas Tech University.

Christmas Concert and dance tradition. Murphey, his band, and the guests who performed with him spread the ideas, concepts, and values associated with the Texas Cowboys' Christmas Ball far beyond Texas and the American Southwest.

Michael Martin Murphey was not alone, of course. Long before he first performed at the Texas Cowboys' Christmas Ball, Jones County citizens had effectively revived the 1880s dance and made it a successful annual pageant. Because of the Star Hotel's fire in circa 1891, Anson citizens discontinued the original dances, but Larry Chittenden's lively, rhyming little poem describing the early events kept the pioneer celebration famous. Moreover, the twenty-seven-year-old Chittenden, who lived several months of each year on his ranch a few miles northwest of Anson, and the Jones County folks, such as John Milsap and Windy Bill Wilkinson, he wrote about served as nearly constant reminders of the 1880s dances.

Texas Cowboys' Christmas Ball dancers in Washington, D.C., 1938. Courtesy of Texas Cowboys' Christmas Ball Association.

A group of Anson folk who carried the Texas Cowboys' Christmas Ball to the National Folk Festival in St. Louis, Missouri, 1947. Courtesy of Texas Cowboys' Christmas Ball Association.

But the fire ended the winter-time dances in Anson—at least on an annual basis. From time to time a Jones County rancher hosted a one- or two-day "blow out," and it is likely someone staged a dance or two in the county courthouse. But the exuberant dances in the Star Hotel and the high-spirited celebrations described by Chittenden—and so different from the courtly, formal soirees of the author's New York City experience—ended.

In 1922, a public folk dance similar to the Cowboy's Christmas Ball occurred in Anson. It was part of a state-wide celebration commemorating the centennial of Stephen Austin's first trip to Texas. Its organizers, led by Leonora Barrett, did not repeat the effort the following year. Minor opposition to rekindling the local dance exposition existed, but larger issues challenging the community in the 1920s turned everyone's attention in other directions.

The twenties were a time of social and cultural change. The decade saw the United States and Texas move more rapidly than ever from rural, agricultural economies to urban, industrial ones. Prohibition and the related crimes it spawned, including bootleg alcohol, plus "speakeasies," jazz music, and flappers in short skirts and painted cheeks with a cigarette dangling from their lips reflected the changing society. Moreover, the failure of the United States to join the League of Nations in the aftermath of World War I complicated the unease, as did the federal government's postwar anti-communist—"Red Scare"—crusade aimed at rooting out communism in America.

For some folks, the cultural changes were unsettling, and they recoiled and resisted. In the early twenties, people in many rural areas of Texas, the Midwest, and the Great Plains encouraged a type of "push-back" against the shifting currents. The Ku Klux Klan, for example, was active in many rural Texas areas; although highly bigoted, its major appeal was to preserve conservative, rural, and Protestant communities like Anson against a growing perceived threat of urban society with its liberal tendencies, Catholicism, and immigrant populations.

In another response to the shifting social and cultural milieu in the 1920s, dancing became less popular in many parts of Texas, including Anson. There may have been only a few flappers in Anson (or more likely none), and many big-city problems seemed far away from Jones County. Yet, conservative evangelical Christianity was popular in the Bible Belt of America, and it may have encouraged the lack of enthusiasm for continuing a big, public dance in the years after 1922. For whatever reasons, the public dance revival did not last.

In 1934, conditions were different. The stock market crash in 1929 and afterward and the Great Depression in the 1930s had set in motion new intellectual and cultural currents. Prohibition ended and much of the crime associated with it disappeared. Economic conditions in the country and in Jones County had not improved, but at long last the nation's mood, spurred in part by President Franklin D. Roosevelt's exuberant optimism, was hopeful again.

Meanwhile, events on a local level had taken an unexpected turn. In 1933, the Anson city council, in a clearly theocratic and short-sighted action, outlawed public dancing in their community—"No Dancin' in Anson," as described in the *Texas Monthly*.[9]

Nonetheless, in 1934 Leonora Barrett could not be denied. A folklorist, author, and English teacher at Anson High School, Barrett determined to hold a "reenactment" of the 1885 dance. A Southerner born in Alabama and an Anson High School graduate, she held a B. A. degree from Southern Methodist University and an M. A. degree from the University of Texas at Austin. She was intensely proud of Texas and its heritage and understood the historical value of Chittenden's poem and the dances it described.[10]

Barrett got help from Hybernia Grace, another Anson High School teacher. Grace taught social studies and as a practicing historian wrote and published articles in both popular and scholarly journals. Indeed, she wrote one of the first serious biographies of Larry Chittenden, an article-length piece that appeared in the *West Texas Historical Association Year Book* in 1937.[11]

Barrett, Grace, and a few others wanted to promote Anson's rich cultural heritage. They sought to re-create an event that "would historically characterize their home town." Reviving the folk dancing described in "The Cowboys' Christmas Ball" seemed appropriate, and they planned for an outdoor festival to take place in the fall of 1934. Late in September, however, they heard that Larry Chittenden had died on the twenty-fourth, and, thereupon, they abandoned "the original plans . . . [in favor of] a memorial folk dance" patterned after the event described by the poet ranchman nearly fifty years earlier.[12]

The women borrowed the high school gymnasium for the event and set a new date for December, on the weekend before Christmas. They decorated the gymnasium with cedar boughs, oak foliage, mesquite branches, and mistletoe. They encouraged participants to dress in 1880s attire and to follow the "rules," at least as they understood the requirements that M. G. Rhoads

Members of the Texas Cowboys' Christmas Ball Association, 1972 or 1973. Courtesy of Texas Cowboys' Christmas Ball Association.

enforced at his Star Hotel. In effect, it would be a reenactment of the first big Anson Christmas-time celebration.[13]

It all worked. For the most part, people did indeed come in 1880s-style clothes. Women wore dresses with high necks, long sleeves, and full shimmering skirts. Men wore jeans, good white shirts, and boots without spurs, and they checked their hats at the door. Musical instruments also reflected the late 1880s—fiddles, a guitar, and a bass viol. Likewise, a recently married couple led the grand march that opened the dance and folk festival.

Leonora Barrett described the 1934 reenactment. The dance opened with a chorus singing the entire Chittenden ballad, a young recently married couple led the grand march, and in "accordance with olden times, the dances used were folk steps of the open range society." The dances, she wrote, included "the schottische, the square, the polka, the old waltz, and the Virginia Reel," a few of the dances that American presidents such as George Washington in New York City and Thomas Jefferson had sponsored in the executive mansion in Washington, D.C. (later known as the White House).[14]

Barrett, Grace, and the other organizers invited back several of the people

Folks associated with the first pre-dance dinner, 1993. Photo by Karen Murphey. Courtesy of Michael Martin Murphey.

who had been at the 1885 dance for another go-round. Many of them came, some of whom had been children, or at least young people, in the 1880s. Walter Wright, one of the fiddle players from the 1880s dances, and Bob Weatherby were among them in 1934.[15]

Over the next few years, Barrett's group continued to invite the 1880s attendees. In 1938, William "Windy Bill" Williamson, the square dance caller mentioned in Chittenden's poem, appeared and "had the time of his life." By 1943, writes Barrett, "virtually every living person who attended the original Ball had returned sometime for the re-enactment, even though living as far away as Arizona and California."[16]

Because of the 1934 success, Barrett, Grace, and their friends decided to hold the dance again. Then, they held it again, and again, every time in the high school gymnasium, which they continued to decorate in much the same style as they had in 1934. They kept the tradition of the grand march, encouraged attendees to wear period clothes, and continued to dance the dances that had been popular back in the 1880s. They staged the reenactment over four evenings on the weekend before Christmas.

The grand event attracted attention. *The New York Times* requested information about the dance, and Anson folk dancers associated with the ball participated in the 1936 Texas Centennial celebration. In June during the year-long celebration, they presented the reenactment in Dallas.[17]

The next year the dancers received an invitation to perform at the National Folk Festival in Chicago. The National Folklore Society, which sponsored the festival, considered the reenactment "an excellent example of folklore" and invited the Anson dancers to perform at their annual meeting and conference. A year later they went to the same event in Washington, D. C., where they danced on the White House lawn. Later, in 1947, another group of Anson dancers carried the Texas Cowboys' Christmas Ball to the National Folk Festival in Saint Louis.[18]

To support the annual reenactments, Barrett and others established the Texas Cowboy's Christmas Ball Association. They incorporated the organization, copyrighted the name of their festival, and wrote a constitution and bylaws. The document of incorporation, which was formally renewed some years later, covered several pages and detailed the purpose and mission of the Association: "To foster interest in folk dancing, to prolong the lore and history of the Old West, and to preserve the cultural history and social development of the American frontier."

Clearly, the national attention, the creation of the Association, and the steps taken to protect the reenactment's name suggest that the Christmas event was enjoying considerable success. Indeed, it was. Despite dress code and related restrictions, the dance drew people from near and far, from both city and ranch. Working cowboys, who rarely removed their hats, attended and appeared on the gymnasium dance floor without their Stetsons and minus their spurs.

Because of the success, the Texas Cowboy's Christmas Ball Association in 1938 sought a venue other than the local gymnasium for its popular dance. The Association hired Andy Sprayberry, a local contractor, for the work and with help from the Works Projects Administration (WPA), one of the Roosevelt administration's agencies designed to put people to work during the Depression, construction began. When finished in 1940, the new building, Pioneer Hall—71 feet wide by 121 feet long, or nearly 8,600 square feet—was ready in time for that year's December dance celebration. Sprayberry and associates designed and built the hall specifically "for the historic panorama." As noted in Chapter 1, Pioneer Hall has been home to the Texas Cowboys' Christmas Ball every year since 1940.[19]

Association members trimmed the interior of Pioneer Hall along the lines of the old Star Hotel. According to Leonora Barrett, they "gaily decorated with balloons, mountain cedar, deer horns and cattle horn relics from the almost forgotten Texas range." They placed colorful "blankets and coverlets on the long walls [to] enhanced the general effect." And, they hung "Russian thistles, glistening with Christmas icicles" on the "heavy beams" and interlaced them "with holiday festooning." And, on opening night the hosts "and hostesses in pioneer costumes of the [1880s and 1890s] station themselves at their posts of duty" at eight o'clock for the beginning of the ball.[20]

Decorations changed some over the years, but cedar and mistletoe remain. Photos of people in attendance through the years hang on the walls, a replica of Larry Chittenden's Jones County ranch house is located in the

The Honor Wall in Pioneer Hall recognizes several former presidents, secretaries, and major leaders of the Texas Cowboys' Christmas Ball Association. Courtesy of Monte L. Monroe.

building, and a Christmas tree in full dress often stands near the entrance. While the idea of maintaining tradition continues, concerns over fire in the building now dictate how Pioneer Hall may be decorated.

In the early 1940s, the Anson dance, as noted, was attracting national attention, even if some locals knew little about it. In 1942, for example, while the nation was engaged in World War II, "guests registered from thirty-four states," writes Leonora Barrett, "many coming from Army camps," and "others visiting relatives somewhere in the West." Soldiers from nearby military bases came to Anson on buses or the train. Their presence in Anson during the war, which wasn't going well for the United States and its Allies at the time, accounts for the large number of states being represented in the register for 1942.

World War II did not stop the Texas Cowboys' Christmas Ball, but did cause Association members to question whether they should continue the

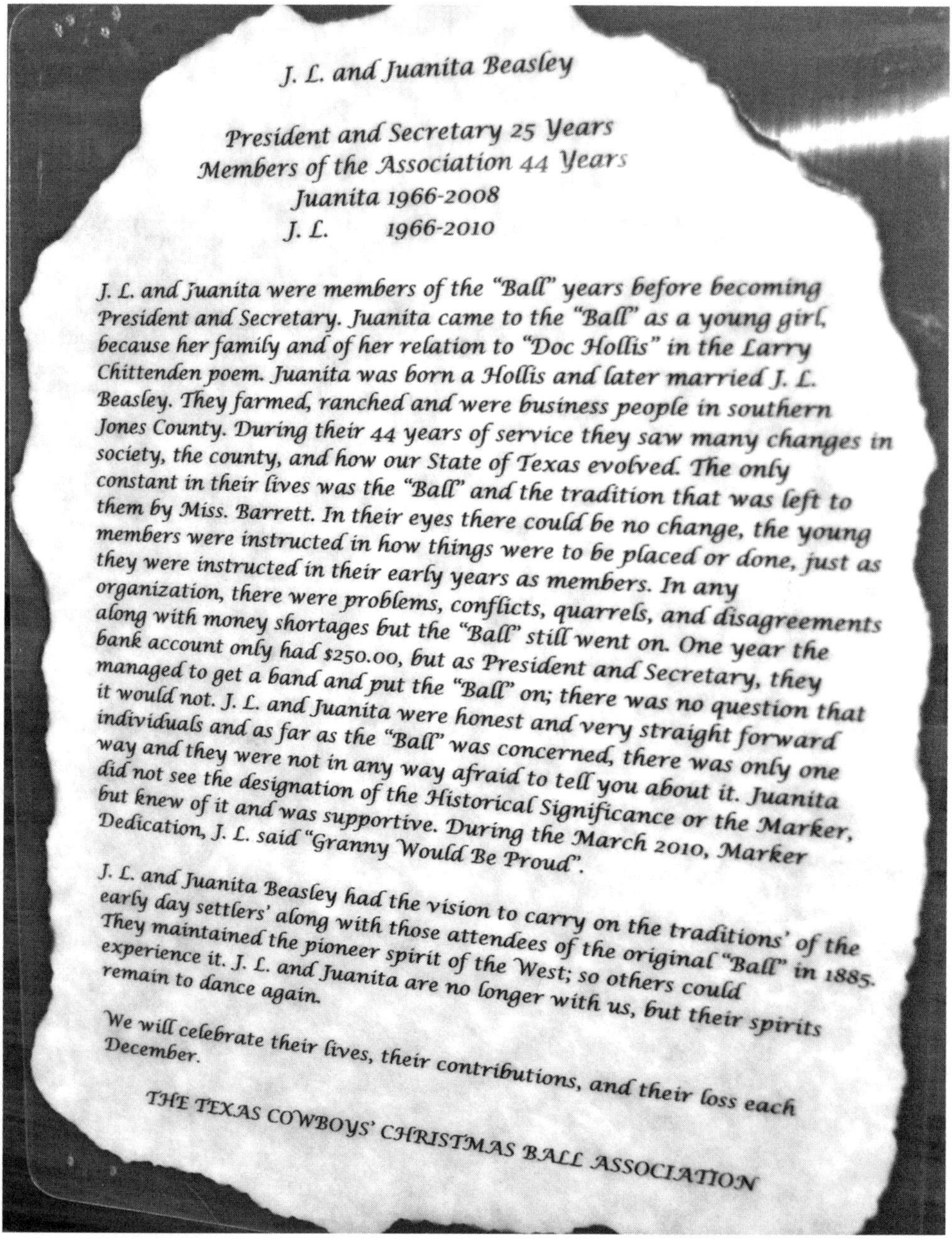

J. L. and Juanita Beasley

President and Secretary 25 Years
Members of the Association 44 Years
Juanita 1966-2008
J. L. 1966-2010

J. L. and Juanita were members of the "Ball" years before becoming President and Secretary. Juanita came to the "Ball" as a young girl, because her family and of her relation to "Doc Hollis" in the Larry Chittenden poem. Juanita was born a Hollis and later married J. L. Beasley. They farmed, ranched and were business people in southern Jones County. During their 44 years of service they saw many changes in society, the county, and how our State of Texas evolved. The only constant in their lives was the "Ball" and the tradition that was left to them by Miss. Barrett. In their eyes there could be no change, the young members were instructed in how things were to be placed or done, just as they were instructed in their early years as members. In any organization, there were problems, conflicts, quarrels, and disagreements along with money shortages but the "Ball" still went on. One year the bank account only had $250.00, but as President and Secretary, they managed to get a band and put the "Ball" on; there was no question that it would not. J. L. and Juanita were honest and very straight forward individuals and as far as the "Ball" was concerned, there was only one way and they were not in any way afraid to tell you about it. Juanita did not see the designation of the Historical Significance or the Marker, but knew of it and was supportive. During the March 2010, Marker Dedication, J. L. said "Granny Would Be Proud".

J. L. and Juanita Beasley had the vision to carry on the traditions' of the early day settlers' along with those attendees of the original "Ball" in 1885. They maintained the pioneer spirit of the West; so others could experience it. J. L. and Juanita are no longer with us, but their spirits remain to dance again.

We will celebrate their lives, their contributions, and their loss each December.

THE TEXAS COWBOYS' CHRISTMAS BALL ASSOCIATION

This plaque located on the wall inside Pioneer Hall honors J. L. and Juanita Beasley, whose combined service to the Christmas Ball totaled half a century. Courtesy of Monte L. Monroe.

dance. The large number of soldiers in attendance each year justified keeping the dance alive, and as the Allies' fortunes improved, their decision to perform the reenactment every December was widely supported in the community.

In the late 1940s and early 1950s, a newscaster for KRBC radio in Abilene conducted live remotes from Pioneer Hall. For radio listeners, the announcer needed to paint a picture with words of the dance and the people in attendance. He described the dancers, the decorations, and the music so people listening over the radio could visualize what was taking place. He sometimes interviewed Association members and mentioned the names of some of the prominent Abilene-area residents in attendance. As television became more popular in the mid to late 1950s, KRBC discontinued the radio broadcasts.[21]

Also in the 1950s, the Texas Cowboys' Christmas Ball became a three-day event. The Association held their dance and reenactment on the Thursday, Friday, and Saturday before Christmas. Over time, the Thursday evening event attracted older couples, who came early, danced hard to the music of Abe Crutchfield's little orchestra or other early house bands, and left well before the evening's end at midnight. The Friday night event evolved into the classic reenactment with attendees dressed in period clothes, while Association members directed the grand march and other manifestations of the 1880s. Saturday evening centered on young people, and Santa Claus appeared in cowboy gear to greet the children. As Nola McKey describes it, he showed up "in a red-and-white jacket, Wranglers, chaps, spurs, and cowboy boots, and carrying saddlebags filled with candy."[22]

From time to time, practical and financial considerations led to changes in each evening's emphasis. In 2013, for example, Christmas ball leaders moved the children's evening to Friday night. They also reestablished the traditional Thursday night emphasis on "old-time" music and dancing. Thus, Saturday became the night of the classic reenactment.

As noted, Gordon Graham, who had recorded "The Cowboy's Christmas Ball" in 1946, sang the musical poem to start that year's dance. In fact, Graham, who was living in Chicago at the end of the 1930s, had been at the 1937 ball; he attended again in 1964, coming from his home in Grand Junction, Colorado. Since Graham's 1946 performance, a chorus or soloist has sung the lively ballad. In the course of the evening, a person also read Larry Chittenden's poem.

Until recently, house bands provided most of the music for the Christmas

Members of Texas Cowboys' Christmas Ball Association, 2004. Courtesy of Texas Cowboys' Christmas Ball Association.

ball. There have been many such groups. Archie Jefferies played with his band in 1954. Bob Burks and the West Texas Wranglers performed in 1965. Abilene's L. C. Agnew and the Dixie Playboys performed at many balls in the 1970s and 1980s, although Leon Rausch and the Texas Panthers provided the music in 1982. Vernon Willingham and the Texas Rhythm Boys played in 1990 and for a few years afterward.[23]

Problems over the years have included financial difficulties and expensive repairs on Pioneer Hall. During the 1950s and into the early 1960s, the ball got a "black eye," so to speak, due to alcohol consumption. The Texas Cowboys' Christmas Ball Association owns Pioneer Hall and the ground around the building. The Association can and does restrict the use of alcohol on its property, but it cannot stop people from imbibing beer, wine, or stronger liquor on property it does not own, such as the nearby city park or the county fairgrounds. The use of alcohol in such places spilled over onto the dance floor, and as a result for a decade or more some folks preferred to stay away from the annual dance.

Suanne Holtman and Bernie Holtman, 2011. Courtesy of Monte L. Monroe.

The dance survived the temporary hit on its reputation. More careful policing, greater affirmation of the dance as a family event, renewed emphasis on its original purpose of fostering interest in folk dancing, and re-creating the 1885 dance that Chittenden described all helped. Where once two or three Anson city policemen maintained a presence, since at least 1995 the ball has not required the presence of law enforcement officers.[24]

Financial problems were another matter: the Association ran the ball on a shoestring budget and shortfalls were common. In the late 1980s, the roof of Pioneer Hall leaked, the front entrance needed upgrading, and due to lack of funds general maintenance and repairs were often delayed.[25]

Then, in 1992, Bernard "Bernie" Holtman became president of the Texas Cowboys' Christmas Ball Association and, with good fortune, his wife Suanne Holtman became secretary. Bernie, a burly former model and oilfield worker and ranch hand from Hawley, about half-way between Anson and Abilene, was a shrewd organizer and a calm, even folksy leader who knew how to push Christmas ball dreams toward reality. Suanne, a former nurse, was a petite, fast-talking burst of energy. Although she had heard of the dance in the 1980s, she did not attend in that period.[26]

Left to right are Karen and Michael Martin Murphey, and the recently married couple who led the grand march in 2011. Courtesy of Monte L. Monroe.

Fortunately, the Holtmans took dancing lessons and attended for the first time about 1990 and have not missed a Texas Cowboys' Christmas Ball since then. As president and secretary, they made a dynamic team. They infused renewed enthusiasm into the Christmas Ball and rejuvenated Association members with new ideas and energy without dismembering dance traditions that had prevailed for nearly sixty years. Their arrival was timely.

Next, Michael Martin Murphey arrived. A native of Dallas, Murphey as a youth spent time on his step-grandfather's ranch in Freestone County, where, according to Nola McKey, "he learned some of the old ballads from cowboys gathered around the campfire." By age sixteen, he had become a singing cowboy, and later in Austin, Texas, he was part of the Willie Nelson-Waylon Jennings, outlaw country-rock scene. Then, upon advice from his mother and Roy Rogers, he changed his act and returned to his country-cowboy roots.[27]

In the 1980s, as noted, Murphey, having renewed his passion for cowboy music and poetry, began performing cowboy Christmas shows. They attracted large crowds. In 1986, he copyrighted the name "Cowboy Christmas" and "The Cowboy Christmas Ball." Also, about this time he founded "WestFest," an annual music festival sometimes held at Copper Mountain Resort in Colorado, as well as in Deadwood, South Dakota, and Rifle, Colorado. Because he wanted to preserve memories and images of the Old West, "WestFest" celebrates and honors western art and culture, too.[28]

By 1992, Murphey writes, he "was on [his] way to being the singing cowboy [he] had wanted to be since [his] childhood."[29] He had also become interested in the Texas Cowboys' Christmas Ball in Anson.

Concomitantly, members of the Cowboys' Christmas Ball Association realized that they had an opportunity to bring Michael Martin Murphey and his Christmas tour to Anson. Bernie Holtman, the brand new president, negotiated with Art Fegan of World Class Entertainment, Murphey's booking agent in Nashville, and signed a contract. Both parties were pleased. "I was overwhelmed," Murphey writes, "because I knew [the Association] was made up of very conservative people from a small ranching community who did not want to risk changing the event into a popular-styled country music concert bash." In fact, Juanita Beasley, who had been secretary of the Association for some twenty-two years, "wasted no time in letting [Murphey] know that [the] Texas Cowboys' Christmas Ball was a revered traditional dance with ironclad rules."[30]

Murphey was a hit. He appeared for the first time in December 1993 and played before a record-setting crowd. More than 850 dancers, the maximum number of people the fire marshal would allow in the building, pushed into Pioneer Hall. They crammed the north-side bleachers and pressed onto the

Michael Martin Murphey's daughter Sarah asleep on the lap of Caroline Mayer after a long night of dancing at the Texas Cowboys' Christmas Ball, 2011. Photo by Michael Martin Murphey. Courtesy of Michael Martin Murphey.

Couple dancing in period dress at the Texas Cowboys' Christmas Ball, 2011. Courtesy of Monte L. Monroe.

dance floor with their chairs and blankets, taking up nearly a third of the dancing area.

Despite the crowded conditions, traditions remained steadfast. The ball began with the grand march around the compressed dancing area. A recently married couple led the march with the guests of honor behind them, followed by every couple at the dance who chose to participate in the march. And, of course, Murphey's Rio Grande band played "The Eyes of Texas" during the march while members of the Association, as in the past, directed traffic as couples in almost military fashion moved about the dance floor. Then, Association members, dressed in their coordinated outfits—men in jeans, white shirts, and black string ties, ladies in long dresses of the same color—danced the Virginia reel as other attendees watched. Afterward everyone participated in the Paul Jones, a round dance in which women and men dancers form two circles. Women form a bigger outside circle and the men the inside circle. Each group joins hands and walks in opposite direc-

Children dancing at the Texas Cowboys' Christmas Ball, 2012. Courtesy of Monte L. Monroe.

tions until a whistle blows. Then each person dances with the person facing him or her.[31]

Dancing continued until midnight. Murphey and his band played schottisches, polkas, waltzes, and popular Texas swing dances. "Cotton-Eyed Joe," "The Rose of San Antone," "Put Your Little Foot" (varsovienne, varsouviana), "Red River Valley," and other traditional songs and favorite dances were all part of the 1993 Christmas celebration. And, as Murphey writes, "Of course, the last waltz of the evening at all traditional cowboy dances is 'Good-bye Old Paint, I'm Leaving Cheyenne.'"[32]

The 1993 Texas Cowboys' Christmas Ball must be judged a grand triumph. Murphey was excited enough that he renewed his contract and for nearly two decades afterward he has participated in the Anson event, with the exception of 2007 when he was ill. In part, his participation allowed him to expand his annual Christmas tour, which by 2003 included ten states and forty cities.

Michael Martin Murphey and daughter Sarah dancing in Pioneer Hall, 2012. Photo by Karen Murphey. Courtesy of Michael Martin Murphey.

Over time, Michael Martin Murphey became indelibly linked to the Anson event. On several occasions, he brought his entire family to Anson, participated in the grand march with his wife Karen, and danced with his daughters before taking to the stage. At the 2012 dance, his daughter Sarah recited cowboy poetry. Murphey quickly came to love the Texas Cowboys' Christmas Ball. It is one of the last stops on his long, annual Christmas tour. According to Nola McKey, Murphey in 2003 said, "As long as the folks in the [Association] want me and I can get on and off the [tour] bus, I plan to keep on playing at the Cowboys' Christmas Ball." He respects the way the Anson dance "is about people keeping their lifestyle going. It's a celebration of a way of life."[33]

For the Association, Murphey's appearance raised badly needed money. After the first two or three years of his participation, the Association could pay its bills, repair the roof of Pioneer Hall, and make a few other physical adjustments, although unfortunately, in 2013 funds were once again at low ebb. Murphey's performances, moreover, provided excitement to the Christmas Ball, added much needed publicity to the event, and attracted younger people to the family dance party.

During Bernie Holtman's tenure as president of the Association (1992–2007) some significant changes occurred. Association leaders added a door at the southwest corner of the dance hall. Holtman gathered and collated a large amount of material in order to write a long narrative for Pioneer Hall's application to the Texas Historical Commission's historical marker program. The application was successful and a marker is now attached to the front of the building. He and Suanne Holtman, with some help from Christmas ball historian Rhonda Weaver, collected six boxes of historical materials relating to the Texas Cowboys' Christmas Ball and sent them to the Southwest Collection/Special Collections Library at Texas Tech University, for preservation and for use by future historians interested in researching, writing, and preserving the life of the ball, history on Anson, and cowboy culture.[34]

Another innovation of the Holtman-Murphey era was the Cowboy Christmas Ranch Supper. The performance contract between Murphey and the Association stipulated that the Association provide a meal for Murphy and his Rio Grande band on the evening they played at the Cowboys' Christmas Ball. The Holtmans in 1993 suggested a covered dish dinner, and by 2009 it had evolved into a large, ranch-style potluck supper served buffet style. The Association invited as many people to the meal as it could accommodate, and charged each of them fifty dollars, the proceeds to be used to rent the building and to raise additional funds for the dance and celebration.[35]

The plan worked very well. Held in the little building across the street from Pioneer Hall, the meal has regularly attracted a full house, thanks to careful planning, close organization, and the hard work of Association members, especially the women. In 2012, Mark and John Compere, and later Curtis Peoples with members of Texas Tech University's music department, provided music on a little stage in the building as people gathered and ate. Michael Martin Murphey, his family, and his band mingled with the crowd. People took plenty of pictures as they and their friends sought to be photographed with Murphey or get him to sign a new cookbook. The food was delicious. The talk was friendly. The ambiance and atmosphere were celebratory. In short, the ranch dinner became a wonderful prelude to the dance that followed.

Michael Martin Murphey, 2013. Photo by Joe Ownbey. Courtesy of Michael Martin Murphey.

The evening meal tradition led to the publication of a ranch dinner cookbook. Designed to raise money for operating the ball, it also helped to promote the dance and provide recipes for food served at the evening's covered-dish dinner. Murphey suggested the idea of creating a cookbook, and in 2010 Suanne Holtman took charge. With help from a number of Association members and Elissa Stroman of Texas Tech University's Southwest Collection, she gathered recipes, organized the book, and found a printer. Ready in time for the 2012 dance, the book sold well and Suanne Holtman soon was considering a second printing.[36]

For six years during Bernie Holtman's presidency of the Association, the Holtmans promoted the Texas Cowboys' Christmas Ball on Harry Holt's Farm and Ranch Show on KRBC TV in Abilene. Holt, who previously had worked for the *Abilene Reporter News* and for KRBC radio, proved an enthusiastic supporter of the ball, and each year he called Bernie to remind him and Suanne to come to Abilene to talk about the Christmas ball on his program. They appeared every year until Holt became ill and discontinued the popular farm program.[37]

The Holtmans were not alone in their efforts, of course. They got help from Association members, enlisted new members, and encouraged them to accept individual responsibility for Christmas Ball activities. Among those who have helped in recent years were Greg and Allison Pinkston. Greg became involved during his tenure as president of the local Chamber of Commerce from 1996 to 2000. He believed that the Chamber and the city needed to participate in the event, for it brought international attention and good business to Anson.[38] Tommie and Cindy Sprayberry, whose relatives have been associated with the ball since Andy Sprayberry built Pioneer Hall, have also been active when personal responsibilities have not turned their attention elsewhere.

In 2006, for example, a wedding occurred on the dance floor. The event was not expected by other dancers and even the house band Lariet. With the aid of Association members, Judge Lee Hamilton of Taylor County married Christeena Gean Brimmell and Eric Raes Whitt, both of Salado in Bell County. The wedding ceremony with special "cowboy" vows that Judge Hamilton had prepared occurred in the center of the dance floor with Brimmell and Whitt family members standing with the couple and everyone else watching and listening to the wonderful event.[39]

Association members clean and wax the Pioneer Hall dance floor. Waxing is a toilsome and little-appreciated chore. The first time they participated in the process, the Holtmans started with thirty, one-pound cans of Johnson's Paste Wax. They began by applying the material by hand. Progress was slow, taking about eight hours to finish only a tiny portion of the floor. Bishop Powell, leader of the house band Lariat, arrived the second evening, but, as with the Holtmans, he found the work arduous. At the end of the evening, Powell became tired enough that he waxed while lying on the floor exhausted. It was an experience he would not forget.

The experience led to more efficient methods. Holtman rented a machine buffer and then improvised on it with materials from home. The rigging worked and he could apply the wax, which in the end totaled fifty-one cans, with the machine. After the wax had dried sufficiently, he used a second machine to buff the floor. The wax application took about thirteen hours, the buffing about five.

In recent years, John Compere and his wife Dolores have been among the most visible Association members. John is a retired brigadier general of the United States Army and former chief judge of the United States Army Court of Military Review, and Dolores is a ranch owner from Baird, Texas. They joined in 2007. Compere, a descendent of the John Milsap character mentioned in Larry Chittenden's poem, has collected memorabilia and related documents connected to Milsap, Chittenden, and the Anson Christmas dance history. Like so many other hard-working members of the Association, such as 2013 president Davis Weaver, Compere was comfortable with cleaning toilets, gathering cedar for decorations, and providing leadership in whatever way may be necessary to ensure the ball's success.[40]

Unfortunately, the future and continuing success of the Texas Cowboys' Christmas Ball remains cloudy. Pioneer Hall is old and in need of repairs, especially a new roof. To save it, some leaders seek to move the building to Texas Tech University's National Ranching Heritage Center. If the building is moved or it can no longer be used, the Texas Cowboys' Christmas Ball Association must find a new venue in Anson. A younger generation of dancers must be attracted to the ball, and the Association must continue to attract leaders with the enthusiasm and dedication of John Compere and Bernie and Suanne Holtman. For the long-term good health of the ball, such challenges must be met in a timely fashion.

Moreover, for the foreseeable future, Michael Martin Murphey must remain interested in the Texas Cowboys' Christmas Ball. As indicated, he and his name are closely linked to the ball. In many ways, he represents the ideal performer—a person of national fame who, like the ball itself, supports and promotes storied traditions and customs of the Old West. On the other hand, the ball is also an important part of Murphey's Christmas concert tour, and, so, in some ways, he needs the ball almost as much as it needs him. Yet, if in the future, Murphey for whatever reasons severs his relationship with the Anson event, the Association will be bruised—at least for a time. The ball once succeeded without an eminent performer. In the twentieth-first century with its cult of celebrity, perhaps another musician with star qualities —but one who will connect with West Texans in the same, natural way Murphey does—might be needed.

The future aside, in 2013, the Association held the modern cowboys' Christmas ball for the seventy-ninth consecutive year, with seventy-three of them in Pioneer Hall. The house band, Muddy Creek, as it has since 2008, played on Thursday and Friday night and opened the ball for Michael

Martin Murphey's performance on Saturday evening. Beyond a few minor adjustments, not much has changed through the years since Leonora Barrett and Hybernia Grace organized the folk dance reenactment nearly eighty years ago.

Clearly, the modern Texas Cowboys' Christmas Ball remains a popular and widely known event. It brings international attention and recognition to Anson and Jones County. Many attendees return each year, with some of them flying to Abilene and renting an automobile for the drive to Anson. Others come in campers, motorhomes, and SUVs from as far away as Minnesota, the Dakotas, Arizona, Maryland, New York, and elsewhere. They spend significant sums of money in Anson, their home for two or three days each December.

Because Association members have remained steadfast in adhering to dance traditions stretching back nearly 130 years, the Texas Cowboys' Christmas Ball remains an exceptional celebration of an Old West–style gala. It continues to be a festive, family-oriented, and historically accurate pageant. It remains traditional and educational, and reenacts a popular pioneer institution. It rekindles romantic but accurate images of the nineteenth-century, western range-cattle industry in Jones County and cowboy life in Anson, Texas, once the tiny, dusty street–dominated, county seat town that served as home to Larry Chittenden's original poem "The Cowboys' Christmas Ball." In short, the modern Texas Cowboys' Christmas Ball is a distinctive, almost mystical event, remarkable for its authentic descriptions and artful portrayals of life on the cattle-ranching frontier of northwest Texas in the 1880s. Let's dance.

Chapter 1

1. See Michael Martin Murphey, "Cowboy Christmas: Anson, Texas Origins to a National Revival, A Brief History and Personal Recollection," *American West Magazine* 1, no. 4 (December 2000–January 2001): 8.
2. Suanne Holtman, letter to Paul Carlson, April 30, 2013, letter in possession of author.
3. Daisey Currie, "The Story of Her Life as Told to Me by Her: The Life Story of Mrs. W. W. Wetsel," 2, transcript, Interview Files, Archives, Panhandle-Plains Historical Museum, Canyon, Texas.
4. Ibid.
5. William Curry Holden, *Alkali Trails or Social and Economic Movements of the Texas Frontier, 1846–1900* (Dallas: Southwest Press, 1930), 165–68.
6. Currie, "The Story of Her Life as Told to Me by Her," 2–3. See also Paul H. Carlson, *Empire Builder in the Texas Panhandle: William Henry Bush*, 29; Holden, *Alkali Trails*, 165–68; Claude Denham, "Frontier Problems and Amusements in Crockett County," *West Texas Historical Association Year Book* 9 (1933): 39; and H. B. Carroll, " Coronado's Step-Children: Social Life in the Early South Plains," *West Texas Historical Association Year Book* 9 (1933): 60–62.
7. Mondel Rogers, *Old Ranches of the Texas Plains*, no. 37; Ron Tyler, et al., *The New Handbook of Texas* (Austin: Texas State Historical Association, 1996), 4: 364.
8. "Program for Cowboys' Ball," *Taylor County News*, March 19, 1886, as cited in Holden, *Alkali Trails*, 167–68. See also Denham, "Frontier Problems and Amusements in Crockett County," 39.

9. *Lubbock Avalanche*, March 6, 1903. See also Holden, *Alkali Trails*, 166–67; and Carroll, "Coronado's Step-Children," 62.
10. Hooper Shelton and Homer Hutto, *First 100 Years in Jones County, Texas* (Stamford, TX: Shelton Press, 1978), 229; quote on 249.
11. Ibid., 36–37, 229, 234.
12. Ibid., 229.
13. Ibid., 46, 250; "The Cowboys' Christmas Ball," Nacogdoches *Daily Sentinel*, December 24, 2011.
14. Holden, *Alkali Trails*, 165.
15. Currie, "The Story of Her Life as Told to Me by Her," 3–5; Carlson, *Empire Builder in the Texas Panhandle*, 28.
16. Shelton and Hutto, *First 100 Years of Jones County, Texas*, 230–31; Homer Hutto and V. Marie Smith, eds., *Jones County Centennial Celebration, 1981* (Anson, TX: Western Observer, 1981), 7.
17. Bernie Holtman, Suanne Holtman, and John Compere, interview by Paul Carlson, April 25, 2013, notes in possession of author.
18. Ibid.
19. Suanne Holtman, interview by Elissa Stroman, October 10, 2011, tape recording, Oral History Collection, Southwest Collection (SWC), Texas Tech University (TTU); "The Cowboys' Christmas Ball," Nacogdoches *Daily Sentinel*, December 24, 2011.
20. Holtman, Holtman, and Compere, interview by Carlson, April 25, 2013.
21. Holtman, interview by Elissa Stroman, October 10, 2011.
22. Juanita Daniel Zachry, "Cowboys' Christmas Ball," in Roy R. Barkley, et al., *The Handbook of Texas Music* (Austin: Texas State Historical Association, 2003), 68. See also Tony Russell, *Country Music Records: A Discography, 1921–1942* (New York: Oxford University Press, 2004), 749.
23. Jamie Aitkin, "No Dancin' in Anson," *Texas Monthly* 14, no. 12 (December 1986): 168, 170; Rhonda Weaver, interview by Monte Monroe, April 16, 2011, Oral History Collection, SWC, TTU. See also John and Judy Deathridge, interview by Curtis Peoples, April 16, 2011, Oral History Collection, SWC, TTU.
24. Holtman, Holtman, and Compere, interview by Carlson, April 25, 2013.
25. Aitkin, "No Dancin' in Anson," 168, 170.
26. Shelton and Hutto, *First 100 Years of Jones County, Texas*, 250.

Chapter 2

1. *Texas Almanac, 2006–2007* (Dallas: *The Dallas Morning News*, 2006), 371; Shelton and Hutto, *The First 100 Years of Jones County, Texas*, 36–37, 229.
2. Shelton and Hutto, *The First 100 Years of Jones County, Texas*, 35.

3. Ibid., 32; Emmett Roberts, "Frontier Experiences of Emmett Roberts," *West Texas Historical Association Year Book* 3 (1927): 47. See also Tyler, et al., *The New Handbook of Texas*, 3: 994–95.
4. See Paul H. Carlson, *The Plains Indians*, 18–19. Quote in Shelton and Hutto, *The First 100 Years of Jones County, Texas*, 33.
5. Shelton and Hutto, *The First 100 Years of Jones County, Texas*, 33.
6. J. Wright Mooar, "Frontier Experiences of J. Wright Moor," *West Texas Historical Association Year Book* 4 (1928): 91–92. See also Joe S. McCombs, "On the Cattle Trail and Buffalo Range, Joe S. McCombs," contributed by Ben O. Grant and J. R. Webb, *West Texas Historical Association Year Book* 11 (1935): 97–101.
7. O. W. Williams, "From Dallas to the Site of Lubbock in 1877," *West Texas Historical Association Year Book* 15 (1939): 8. See also McCombs, "On the Cattle Trail and Buffalo Range, Joe S. McCombs," 97–101.
8. Roberts, "Frontier Experiences of Emmett Roberts," 47.
9. Ibid.
10. Ibid.; Shelton and Hutto, *The First 100 Years of Jones County, Texas*, 34.
11. Mary Whatley Clarke, *The Swenson Saga and the SMS Ranches* (Austin, TX: Jenkins Publishing Company, 1976), 17–18, 131–32; Shelton and Hutto, *The First 100 Years of Jones County, Texas*, 40, 43–45; Tyler, et al., *The New Handbook of Texas*, 175, 176.
12. Shelton and Hutto, *The First 100 Years of Jones County, Texas*, 47–50.
13. Ibid., 49.
14. Ibid., 49–50, quote on p. 50.
15. Minutes, Commissioners' Court, Jones County, vol. I, p. 1, as cited in ibid., 37.
16. Shelton and Hutto, *The First 100 Years of Jones County, Texas*, 35–36.
17. Tyler, et al., *The New Handbook of Texas*, 3: 994–95; *Texas Almanac, 2006–2007*, 254.
18. Tyler, et al., *The New Handbook of Texas*, 1: 193; Shelton and Hutto, *The First 100 Years of Jones County, Texas*, 229–30.
19. Shelton and Hutto, *The First 100 Years of Jones County, Texas*, 229–31.
20. Ibid., 231.
21. Clarke, *The Swenson Saga and the SMS Ranches*, 131–32.
22. Shelton and Hutto, *The First 100 Years of Jones County, Texas*, 230–31.
23. Ibid.
24. *Texas Almanac, 2012–2013*, 254; Holden, *Alkali Trails*, 187–88; Tyler, et al., *The New Handbook of Texas*, 1: 475–76; 3: 434; and 6: 54–55.
25. See Becky Davidson, "Transcending the Moment: Anson's "The Cowboys' Christmas Ball," *West Texas Historical Association Year Book* 78 (2002): 117; Shelton and Hutto, *The First 100 Years of Jones County, Texas*, 45.

26. *Texas Almanac, 2012–2013*, 328.
27. "Larry Chittenden, the 'Poet Ranchman,' and His Texas Ranch," *The Pittsburgh Press*, November 27, 1901.
28. Ibid.
29. Ibid.; "Solitude," *The New York Sun*, February 25, 1883.

Chapter 3

1. "Cowboys' Christmas Ball," *Texas Western* (Anson), June 19, 1890; "Cowboys' Christmas Ball," *Galveston Daily News*, December 27, 1891; "Cowboys' Christmas Ball," *Dallas Morning News*, December 27, 1891. See also Hybernia Grace, "Larry Chittenden and West Texas," *West Texas Historical Association Year Book* 13 (1937): 6. The Chittenden will is in Deed Records, Jones County, Texas, Book 196 (1934–1935), 504–508.
2. "Larry Chittenden and His Autograph Library," *Frontier Times* 11, no. 1 (October 1933): 38; "'Larry' Chittenden, Our 'Poet Ranchman of Texas,'" *Montclair-Glen Ridge Bulletin*, November 8, 1930; "Christmas Cove and the Autograph Library, *Bath* (Maine) *Daily Times and Weekly Independent*, August 20, 1930.
3. Grace, "Larry Chittenden and West Texas," 3.
4. Ibid., 3–4; "Chittenden, William Lawrence (Larry)," in James T. White, ed., *The National Cyclopaedia of American Biography* (New York: J. T. White, Co., 1937), 16: 404; *History of Cincinnati and Hamilton County, Ohio* (Cincinnati: S. B. Nelson & Company, 1894), 481.
5. The poem is "To the Memory of Major Daniel Gano," in Larry Chittenden, *Ranch Verses*, 177–78. See also Federal Works Agency, *Cincinnati: A Guide to the Queen City and Its Neighbors* (Cincinnati: Ohio State Archaeological and Historical Society, 1943), 475.
6. Grace, "Larry Chittenden and West Texas," 4.
7. "Chittenden, William Lawrence (Larry)," *The National Cyclopaedia of American Biography*, 404.
8. Ibid.
9. Ibid.; "Chittenden, Simeon B.," in *The National Cyclopaedia of American Biography*, 34: 400; "Chittenden, Thomas," in James T. White, ed., *The National Cyclopaedia of American Biography* (New York: J. T. White, 1924), 8: 312–13; and "Chittenden, Martin," in ibid., 315.
10. "Chittenden, William Lawrence (Larry)," in *The National Cyclopaedia of American Biography*, 16: 404; Jim Bob Tinsley, *He Was Singin' This Song* (Gainesville: University Press of Florida, 1981), 145; Robbie M. Powers, "Larry Chittenden —A Bard of the Texas Range," *The Cattleman* 16, no. 7 (December 1929): 15, 17–18; Grace, "Larry Chittenden in West Texas," 3–8; "Larry Chittenden, the

'Poet Ranchman' and His Texas Ranch," *The Pittsburgh Press*, November 27, 1901.

11. See Charles H. Tompkins, "A Letter About Larry Chittenden's Poem," *The Cattleman* 39, no. 8 (January 1953): 196–97; Tinsley, *He Was Singin' This Song*, 146.
12. Cited in Tinsley, *He Was Singin' This Song*, 146; Grace, "Larry Chittenden and West Texas," 4.
13. See, for example, Terry G. Jordan, *North American Cattle-Ranching Frontiers*, 237–38; Walter Prescott Webb, *The Great Plains*, 237–40; Frederick W. Rathjen, *The Texas Panhandle Frontier*, 189–91. Perhaps the best brief description of the boom-and-bust nature of open-range ranching in Texas is Randolph B. Campbell, *Gone to Texas: A History of the Lone Star State* (New York: Oxford University Press, 2003), 301–304.
14. "XIT Ranch," in Ron Tyler, et al., *The New Handbook of Texas*, 6: 1101–1102; "Matador Land and Cattle Company" and "Matador Ranch," in ibid., 4: 553–55; James Cox, *Historical and Biographical Record of the Cattle Industry and the Cattlemen of Texas and Adjacent Territory*, 369; Grace, "Larry Chittenden and West Texas," 3–8; Becky Davidson, "Transcending the Moment: Anson's 'The Cowboys' Christmas Ball,'" *West Texas Historical Association Year Book* 78 (2002): 112–26.
15. Deed Records, Jones County, Texas, Book 12 (1890), 328.
16. Grace, "Larry Chittenden and West Texas," 4–5, 8; the Brittain quote is cited in Cox, *Historical and Biographical Record of the Cattle Industry and the Cattlemen of Texas and Adjacent Territory* (St. Louis, MO: Woodward and Tiernan Printing Co., 1895), 369.
17. "Chittenden, William Lawrence (Larry)," *The National Cyclopaedia of American Biography* 16 (1937): 404.
18. Shelton and Hutto, *The First 100 Years of Jones County, Texas*, 42.
19. Tompkins, "A Letter About Larry Chittenden's Poem," 196.
20. William Lawrence Chittenden, *Bermuda Verses* (New York: G. P. Putnam's Sons, 1909), 54–58.
21. Grace, "Larry Chittenden and West Texas," 4–5. See also Tinsley, *He Was Singin' This Song*, 146. There is a photo of the room in Cox, *Historical and Biographical Record of the Cattle Industry*, 369.
22. Grace, "Larry Chittenden and West Texas," 5.
23. Ibid., 5–6.
24. David Foute Eagleton, ed., *Writers and Writings of Texas* (New York: Broadway Publishing Company, 1913), 99–102.
25. Michael Hoinski, "The Drop Everything List," *Texas Monthly* 38, no. 12 (December 2010): 21. See also Michael Martin Murphey, "Cowboy Christmas:

Anson, Texas Origins to a National Revival, A Brief History and Personal Recollection," *American West Magazine* 1, no. 4 (December 2000–January 2001): 8–9; Becky Davidson, "The Story Behind the Legendary Poem," *Lubbock Magazine* 3, no. 12 (December 1997): 11–12; Nola McKey, "The Texas Cowboys' Christmas Ball," *Texas Highways* 50 (December 2003): 40–45.

26. Each of the four reviews cited, plus some forty-six others, are listed without a publication date in the fifth printing (1898) of Larry Chittenden, *Ranch Verses*, 191–95.
27. For examples of writers referring to a book titled *Lafferty's Letters*, see "Chittenden, William Lawrence (Larry)," *The National Cyclopaedia of American Biography* 16 (1937): 404; "Chittenden, William Lawrence," in Tyler, et al., *The New Handbook of Texas*, 6: 92.
28. John A. Lomax, "William Lawrence Chittenden," in Edwin Anderson Alderman, Joel Chandler Harris, and Charles William Kent, eds. and comps., *Library of Southern Literature* (Atlanta: Martin & Hoyt Company, 1907, 1909), 2: 824–25.
29. See Chittenden, *Ranch Verses*, 191–95; Eagleton, ed., *Writers and Writings of Texas*, 10–11, 13, 14, 99; "Larry Chittenden, the 'Poet Ranchman,' and His Texas Ranch," *The Pittsburgh Press*, November 27, 1901; Cox, *Historical and Biographical Record of the Cattle Industry and Cattlemen of Texas and Adjacent Territory*, 369.
30. Eagleton, ed., *Writers and Writings of Texas*, 10–11, 13.
31. McKey, "The Texas Cowboys' Christmas Ball," 42.
32. Walter Prescott Webb, *The Great Plains* (New York: Grosset & Dunlap, 1931), 256–57.
33. "Chittenden, William Lawrence (Larry)," *The National Cyclopaedia of American Biography* 16 (1937): 404.
34. Chittenden, *Bermuda Verses*, 44.
35. "Coaching to Bermuda," *The New York Times*, January 14, 1912.
36. "Chittenden, William Lawrence (Larry)," *The National Cyclopaedia of American Biography* 16 (1937): 404; "Christmas Cove and the Autograph Library," *Bath* (Main) *Daily Times and Weekly Independent*, August 20, 1930; "'Larry' Chittenden, Our 'Poet Ranchman of Texas,'" *Montclair-Glen Ridge Bulletin*, November 8, 1930.
37. See, for example, William E. Leuchtenburg, *The Perils of Prosperity, 1914–1932* (Chicago: University of Chicago Press, 1958), 184; Frederick Lewis Allen, *Only Yesterday: An Informal History of the 1920s* (New York: Harper & Row Publishers, 1931; reprint 1964), 225–40; and George E. Mowry, ed., *The Twenties: Ford, Flappers & Fanatics*, 33–38. See also Deed Records, Jones County, Texas, Book 196 (1934–1935), 504–508.

38. "Larry Chittenden and His Autograph Library," *Frontier Times* 11, no. 1 (October 1933): 37–42.
39. Ibid. See also "Christmas Cove and the Autograph Library," *Bath* (Maine) *Daily Times and Weekly Independent*, August 20, 1930; "'Larry' Chittenden, Our 'Poet Ranchman of Texas,'" *Montclair-Glen Ridge Bulletin*, November 8, 1930.
40. Deed Records, Jones County, Texas, Book 196 (1934–1935), 504–508.

Chapter 4

1. *See* Becky Davidson, "Transcending the Moment: Anson's 'The Cowboys' Christmas Ball," *West Texas Historical Association Year Book* 78 (2002): 112–26.
2. Shelton and Hutto, *First 100 Years of Jones County, Texas*, 35–37. See also Ron Tyler, et al., eds., *The New Handbook of Texas*, 1: 193.
3. Eagleton, ed., *Writers and Writings of Texas*, 11. See also Lucy Lockwood Hazard, *The Frontier in American Literature*, xvi–xx; and David Hackett Fischer, *Albion's Seed: Four British Folkways in America* (New York: Oxford University Press, 1989), 207–418.
4. Davidson, "Transcending the Moment," 112.
5. See David Stanley and Elaine Thatcher, eds., *Cowboy Poets and Cowboy Poetry* (Urbana: University of Illinois Press, 2000), 7, 64–66; John A. Lomax, "William Lawrence Chittenden," in Alderman, Harris, and Kent, eds. and comps., *Library of Southern Literature* 2: 823–27; and Webb, *The Great Plains*, 456–59.
6. N. Howard "Jack" Throp, comp., *Songs of the Cowboys*, 62–67; John A. Lomax, *Cowboy Songs and Other Frontier Ballads*, rev. and enl. (New York: Sturgis and Walton Company, 1916), 85.
7. Holtman, Holtman, and Compere, interview by Paul Carlson, April 25, 2013, notes in possession of author.
8. Davidson, "Transcending the Moment," 116; Shelton and Hutto, *First 100 Years of Jones County*, 32–33; H. C. Carr and M. P. Carr, Memories of Jones County when they arrived in 1879, compiled by M. P. Carr, January 5, 1930, in Southwest Collection (SWC), Texas Tech University (TTU).
9. Davidson, "Transcending the Moment," 116.
10. Ibid., 117.
11. Mrs. Lucien Keene, Hamlin, Texas, to [Leonora Barrett, Anson], n.d., Letters collected by Leonora Barrett, Anson Public Library (hereafter Keene to Barrett, n.d.), as cited in Davidson, "Transcending the Moment," 117.
12. Mike Cox, *West Texas Tales* (Charleston, SC: History Press, 2011), 93–94; Davidson, "Transcending the Moment," 117–18; Holden, *Alkali Trails*, 172.
13. Quotes in Davidson, "Transcending the Moment," 118; Shelton and Hutto, *First 100 Years in Jones County, Texas*, 293; Holtman, Holtman, and Compere, interview by Carlson, April 25, 2013.

14. See, for example, Daisey Currie, "The Story of Her Life as Told to Me by Her: The Life Story of Mrs. W. W. Wetsel," 2–3, transcript, Interview Files, Archives, Panhandle-Plains Historical Museum, Canyon, Texas. See also Holden, *Alkali Trails*, 165; and Paul H. Carlson, *Empire Builder in the Texas Panhandle: William Henry Bush*, 29. Quote in Davidson, "Transcending the Moment," 119.
15. Keene to Barrett, n.d., as cited in Davidson, "Transcending the Moment," 120, 125. See also "That Lively Gaited Sworray the Cowboys' Christmas Ball," pamphlet, n.d., Anson, Texas: Cowboys' Christmas Ball Association, Reference File, SWC, TTU; and Palace Hotel, Abilene, Guest Register, 1890, in possession of John Compere, Baird, Texas.
16. "The Cowboys' Christmas Ball," Nacogdoches *Daily Sentinel*, December 24, 2011; Davidson, "Transcending the Moment," 120.
17. See Holden, *Alkali Trails*, 165; Keene to Barrett, n.d., as cited in Davidson, "Transcending the Moment," 120; Carlson, *Empire Builder in the Texas Panhandle*, 29.
18. Charles A. Jones, "Paradoxical Jones," The Memories of Charles Adam Jones, typescript, February 15, 1933, 230, 236, Clifford B. Jones Papers, 1814–1973, and undated, Box 33 (S 499.1), SWC, TTU; Clarke, *The Swenson Saga and the SMS Ranches*, 17, 131–32. See also Tyler, et al., *The New Handbook of Texas*, 6: 175–77.
19. See Davidson, "Transcending the Moment," 121–22.
20. Mr. and Mrs. Kenneth Cox, interview by Paul Davidson, May 23, 1996, as cited in ibid., 121–22, 126; Clarke, *The Swenson Saga and the SMS Ranches*, 132.
21. Charles H. Tompkins, "A Letter About Larry Chittenden's Poem," *The Cattleman* 39, no. 8 (January 1953): 196.
22. Tyler, et al., *The New Handbook of Texas*, 2: 545.
23. Keene to Barrett, n.d., as cited in Davidson, "Transcending the Moment," 122, 126, n. 24.
24. See John A. Lomax, *Songs of the Cattle Trail and Cow Camp* (New York: Macmillan Company, 1919; reprint, 1927), 109–11, 120–21.
25. William G. Doty, *Myth: A Handbook* (Westport, CT: Greenwood Press, 2004), 43.
26. Davidson, "Transcending the Moment," 122.
27. Tompkins, "A Letter About Larry Chittenden's Poem," 197.
28. Ibid.
29. "Pioneer Physicians Operated Under Difficulties," *Abilene Reporter-News*, April 14, 1929, as cited in ibid., 123.
30. Davidson, "Transcending the Moment," 124; Shelton and Hutto, *First 100 Years of Jones County, Texas*, 49.

31. Shelton and Hutto, *First 100 Years of Jones County, Texas*, 40.
32. Ibid., 34; David J. Murrah, *The Pitchfork Land and Cattle Company: The First Century* (Lubbock: Texas Tech University Press, 1983), 31; David J. Murrah to Paul Carlson, March 26, 2013, letter in possession of author.
33. Eagleton, ed., *Writers and Writings of Texas*, 103–105; Tinsley, *He Was Singin' This Song*, 146–47. Another poem that mentions Windy Bill is "Gettin' Back to the Ranch," a poem that describes Chittenden himself returning to his Jones County ranch after a long absence, and Bill, in the poem at least, is the ranch cook and one of the favored employees.
34. Davidson, "Transcending the Moment," 125.

Chapter 5

1. David Stanley, "Cowboy Poetry Then and Now: An Overview," in Stanley and Thatcher, eds., *Cowboy Poets and Cowboy Poetry*, 3.
2. Hal Cannon, "Cowboy Poetry: A Poetry of Exile," in ibid., 65–66; John A. Lomax and Alan Lomax, *Cowboy Songs and Other Frontier Ballads*. Rev. and enl. ed. (New York: Macmillan Company, 1941), xv–xvi.
3. Lysius Gough, *Western Travels and Other Rhymes* (Dallas: A. D. Aldridge & Co., 1886); H. Allen Anderson, "Gough, Lysius," Ron Tyler, et al., *The New Handbook of Texas*, 3: 256–57; Boone McClure, "Lysius Gough," *Panhandle-Plains Historical Review* 19 (1946): 29–34; B. Byron Price, "Foreword: "Ghosts and Cowboys: Buck Ramsey and the Cowboy Poetry Tradition," in Scott Braucher and Bette Ramsey, eds., *Buck Ramsey's Grass with Essays on his Life and Work* (Lubbock: Texas Tech University Press, 2005), ix–x.
4. The poetry may be pedestrian, but reviewers were exceptional in their praise of the book and *Ranch Verses* was an extraordinary commercial success. See Larry Chittenden, *Ranch Verses* (1898), 191–95.
5. Guy Logsdon, "The Tradition of Cowboy Poetry," in Stanley and Thatcher, eds., *Cowboy Poets and Cowboy Poetry*, 57.
6. Lomax and Lomax, *Cowboy Songs and Other Frontier Ballads*, xxvi, xxviii, xxx.
7. Logsdon, "The Tradition of Cowboy Poetry," 57; Lomax, *Songs of the Cattle Trail and Cow Camp*, 27, 59, 109, 184.
8. Lomax, *Songs of the Cattle Trail and Cow Camp*, 71–73.
9. Cannon, "Cowboy Poetry: A Poetry of Exile," 66.
10. Katie Lee, "Gail Gardner and the Sierry Petes," *Journal of Arizona History* 15, no. 3 (Autumn 1974): 218–19; Hal Cannon, *Rhymes of the Ranges: A New Collection of the Poems of Bruce Kiskaddon*, 1, 4, 5.
11. Cannon, "Cowboy Poetry: A Poetry of Exile," 66–67.
12. Stanley, "Cowboy Poetry Then and Now," in Stanley and Thatcher, eds., *Cowboy Poets and Cowboy Poetry*, 9.

13. See Austin Fife and Alta Fife, eds., *Ballads of the Great West* (Palo Alto, CA: American West Company, 1970), 11, 24–26; Lomax and Lomax, *Cowboy Songs and Other Frontier Ballads*, xviii, xxiv, xxv; Larry Chittenden, *Ranch Verses* (1898), 191–95.
14. Austin and Fife, eds., *Ballads of the Great West*, 24–30.
15. Cannon, "Cowboy Poetry: A Poetry of Exile," 64.
16. A perceptive and lucid essay on poetry and its place in the modern world is Dana Gioia's "Can Poetry Matter?" in Robert McDowell, ed., *Cowboy Poetry Matters, From Abilene to the Mainstream: Contemporary Cowboy Writing* (Ashland, OR: Story Line Press, 2000), 219–38.
17. Fife and Fife, eds., *Ballads of the Great West*, 25. Quote in Nancy Mclelland, "Borderlands: Cowboy Poetry and the Literary Cannon," in McDowell, ed., *Cowboy Poetry Matters, From Abilene to the Mainstream*, 203. See also Lomax, *Songs of the Cattle Trail and Cow Camp*, ix.
18. Stanley, "Cowboy Poetry Then and Now: An Overview," 14.
19. Ibid.
20. Ibid., 15.
21. Bernie Holtman, interview by Paul Carlson, April 25, 2013, notes in possession of author; Becky Davidson, "The Story Behind the Legendary Poem," *Lubbock Magazine* 3, no. 12 (December 1997): 12; Anson *Western Observer*, December 17, 1992.
22. Lomax and Lomax, *Cowboy Songs and Other Frontier Ballads*, 28.
23. Ibid., xv–xvii; quotes in Joseph G. McCoy, *Historic Sketches of the Cattle Trade of the West and Southwest* (Lincoln: University of Nebraska Press, 1985), 167; and Will James, *Cow Country* (New York: Charles Scribner's Sons, 1927), 89.
24. James, *Cow Country*, 89.
25. Shelton and Hutto, *First 100 Years of Jones County, Texas*, 46, 249–50; Daisey Currie, "The Story of Her Life as Told to Me by Her," 2–10.
26. McCoy, *Historic Sketches of the Cattle Trade of the West and Southwest*, 209; Edward Everett Dale, *Cow Country* (Norman: University of Oklahoma Press, 1942; reprint, 1965), 145. See also Guy Logsdon, "The Cowboys' Bawdy Music," in Charles W. Harris and Buck Rainey, eds., *The Cowboy: Six-Shooters, Songs, and Sex* (Norman: University of Oklahoma Press, 1976), 133.
27. Logsdon, "The Cowboys' Bawdy Music," 132–33.
28. Vanita Parrett, "Cowboy Dance Calls," in Mody C. Boatright and Donald Day, eds., *Backwoods to Border* (Dallas: Southern Methodist University Press, 1943), 115; Philip Ashton Rollins, *The Cowboy: An Unconventional History of Civilization on the Old-Time Cattle Range*, rev. and enl. ed. (Norman: University of Oklahoma Press, 1997), 189.

29. J. R. Craddock, "The Cowboy Dance," as cited in Parrett, "Cowboy Dance Calls," 116.
30. Charles H. Tompkins, "A Letter About Larry Chittenden's Poem," *The Cattleman* 39, no. 8 (January 1953): 197.
31. Parrett, "Cowboy Dance Calls," 117.
32. Betty Casey, *Dance Across Texas* (Austin: University of Texas Press, 1985), 16–17.
33. Ibid., 18.
34. Suanne Holtman, interview by Elissa Stroman, October 10, 2011, tape recording, Oral History Collection, Southwest Collection, Texas Tech University.
35. Ibid. See also Casey, *Dance Across Texas*, 15–16.

Chapter 6

1. Michael Martin Murphey, "Cowboy Christmas: Anson, Texas Origins to a National Revival: A Brief History and Personal Recollection," *American West Magazine* 1, no. 4 (December 2000–January 2001): 9.
2. Ibid., 11.
3. Ibid.
4. Nola McKey, "The Texas Cowboys' Christmas Ball," *Texas Highways* 50 (December 2003): 43.
5. Murphey, "Cowboy Christmas," 9–12.
6. Michael Martin Murphey to Paul Carlson, May 22, 2013, letter in possession of author.
7. Murphey, "Cowboy Christmas: Anson, Texas Origins to a National Revival: A Brief History and Personal Recollection," 12.
8. Murphey to Carlson, May 22, 2013.
9. Jamie Aitkin, "No Dancin' in Anson," *Texas Monthly* 14, no. 12 (December 1986): 168. See also Ricardo C. Ainslie, *No Dancin' in Anson: An American Story of Race and Social Change* (Northvale, NJ: Janson Aronson Inc., 1995), 19–21, 32–34, 56–58, 61.
10. TCCB Association, *The Texas Cowboys' Christmas Ball: Ranch Supper Cookbook*, iv–v; Bernie Holtman, interview by Paul Carlson, April 25, 2013, notes in possession of author. Leonora Barrett published a novel, *So Green the Pastures*, in early 1955 shortly before her death in April.
11. Hybernia Grace, "Larry Chittenden and West Texas," *West Texas Historical Association Year Book* 13 (1937): 3–8.
12. Leonora Barrett, "The Story of Folk Dancing at the Chittenden Cowboys' Christmas Ball," *The Southwest Musician* 10, no. 1 (September–October 1943): 19, 22.

13. Becky Davidson, "The Story Behind the Legendary Poem," *Lubbock Magazine* 3, no. 12 (December 1997); 11–12; Jim Bob Tinsley, *He Was Singin' This Song*, 147; "The Cowboys' Christmas Ball," Nacogdoches *Daily Sentinel*, December 24, 2011; Murphey, "Cowboy Christmas," 9.
14. Barrett, "The Story of Folk Dancing at the Cowboys' Christmas Ball."
15. Ibid.
16. Ibid.
17. Ibid.; Barrett, "The Story of Folk Dancing at the Cowboys' Christmas Ball," *The Southwest Musician* 10, no. 1 (September–October 1943): 19, 22; Hybernia Grace, "Larry Chittenden and West Texas," *West Texas Historical Association Year Book* 13 (1937): 6; "That Lively Gaited Sworray the Cowboys' Christmas Ball," pamphlet, n.d., in Anson, Texas: Cowboys' Christmas Ball Association, Reference File, SWC, TTU. See also McKey, "The Texas Cowboys' Christmas Ball," 43–44.
18. Barrett. "The Story of Folk Dancing at the Cowboys' Christmas Ball," pamphlet, n.d., in Anson, Texas: Cowboys' Christmas Ball Association, Reference File, SWC, TTU. See also, "That Lively Gaited Sworray the Cowboys' Christmas Ball," in Ibid.
19. Bernie Holtman, Suanne Holtman, and John Compere, interview by Paul Carlson, April 25, 2013, notes in possession of author; quote in Barrett, "The Story of Folk Dancing at the Chittenden Cowboys' Christmas Ball," pamphlet, n.d., in Anson, Texas: Cowboys' Christmas Ball Association, Reference File, SWC, TTU. See also the Texas State historical marker, dated 2003, on the front of the building. While the building was 8,600 square feet in size, the dance floor was smaller—closer to 8,400 square feet, as noted in chapter 1.
20. Quotes in Barrett, "The Story of Folk Dancing at the Chittenden Cowboys' Christmas Ball," pamphlet, n.d., in Anson, Texas: Cowboys' Christmas Ball Association, Reference File, SWC, TTU.
21. Holtman, Holtman, and Compere, interview by Carlson, April 25, 2013.
22. McKey, "The Texas Cowboys' Christmas Ball," 42.
23. Joe Carr and Alan Munde, *Prairie Nights to Neon Lights: The Story of Country Music in West Texas* (Lubbock: Texas Tech University Press, 1997), 196.
24. Holtman, interview by Carlson, April 25, 2013. See also K. A. Gouza and Mavalyn, interview by Curtis Peoples, April 16, 2011, tape recording, Oral History Collection, SWC, TTU.
25. Holtman, Holtman, and Compere, interview by Carlson, April 25, 2013.
26. Suanne Holtman, interview by Elissa Stroman, October 10, 2011, tape recording, Oral History Collection, SWC, TTU.
27. Quote in McKey, "The Texas Cowboys' Christmas Ball," 43.

28. Murphey, "Cowboy Christmas," 11.
29. Ibid.
30. Holtman, interview by Carlson, April 25, 2013; quotes in Murphey, "Cowboy Christmas," 11.
31. Holtman, Holtman, and Compere, interview by Carlson, April 25, 2013; Murphey, "Cowboy Christmas," 11–12.
32. Murphey, "Cowboy Christmas," 12.
33. McKey, "The Texas Cowboys' Christmas Ball," 43.
34. Holtman, interview by Carlson, April 25, 2013.
35. Holtman, Holtman, and Compere, interview by Carlson, April 25, 2013.
36. Ibid.
37. Ibid.
38. Greg Pinkston, interview by Monte Monroe, August 16, 2011, tape recording, Oral History Collection, SWC, TTU.
39. Suanne Holtman, letter to Paul Carlson, June 15, 2013, letter in possession of author.
40. Holtman, Holtman, and Compere, interview by Carlson, April 25, 2013.

BIBLIOGRAPHY

Manuscript Sources

Anson, Texas: Cowboys' Christmas Ball Association, Reference File. Southwest Collection, Texas Tech University.

Barrett, Leonora. "Evolution of Plains Literature." Unpublished manuscript, no date. Public Library, Anson.

———. "The Texas Cowboy in Literature." Master's thesis, University of Texas, 1930.

Currie, Daisey. "The Story of Her Life as Told to Me by Her: The Life Story of Mrs. W. W. Wetsel." Transcript in Interview Files, Archives, Panhandle-Plains Historical Museum, Canyon, Texas.

Holtman, Bernard. "Remembrances of Texas Cowboys' Christmas Ball," 2001–2007, 2009–2012. In possession of Bernard Holtman, Hawley, Texas.

Holtman, Suanne. Letter to Paul Carlson, April 30, 2013. Letter in possession of author.

———. Letter to Paul Carlson, June 16, 2013. Letter in possession of author.

Jones, Clifford B. Papers, 1814-1—973, and undated. Box 33 (S499.1). Southwest Collection, Texas Tech University.

Lewis, Cheryl. Letter to Paul Carlson, June 8, 2013. Letter in possession of author.

Murphey, Michael Martin. Letter to Monte L. Monroe, May 22, 2013. Letter in possession of author.

———. Letter to Paul Carlson, May 22, 2013. Letter in possession of author.

Murrah, David J. Letter to Paul Carlson, March 26, 2013. Letter in possession of author.

Palace Hotel, Abilene. Guest Register, 1890. In possession of John Compere, Baird, Texas.

Swenson, Gail. "S. M. Swenson and the Development of the SMS Ranches." Master's thesis, University of Texas, 1960.

Texas Cowboys' Christmas Ball Manuscripts. 6 boxes. Crossroads of Music Archives. Southwest Collection, Texas Tech University.

Government Documents

Jones County, Texas. *Deed Records.* 1892, Book 12; 1903, Book 26; 1907, Book 46; 1929, Book 167; 1934, Book 196. Jones County Courthouse, Anson, Texas.

———. *General Index of Deed Records.* 1881–1894; 1903–1907; 1907–1908; 1910–1923; 1927–1932; 1933–1935. Jones County Courthouse, Anson, Texas.

Interviews

Deathridge, Clay. Interview by Monte Monroe, April 16, 2011, tape recording in Oral History Collection, Southwest Collection, Texas Tech University.

Deathridge, John and Judy. Interview by Curtis Peoples. April 16, 2011. Tape recording, Oral History Collection. Southwest Collection, Texas Tech University.

Dokey, Jimmy. Interview by Curtis Peoples, April 16, 2011, tape recording, Oral History Collection, Southwest Collection, Texas Tech University.

Gouza, K. A. and Mavalyn. Interviewed by Curtis Peoples, April 16, 2011, tape recording, Oral History Collection, Southwest Collection, Texas Tech University.

Holtman, Bernie. Interview by Paul Carlson, April 25, 2013, notes in possession of author.

Holtman, Bernie, Suanne Holtman, and John Compere. Interview by Paul Carlson, April 25, 2013, notes in possession of author.

Holtman, Suanne. Interview by Elissa Stroman, October 10, 2011, tape recording, Oral History Collection, Southwest Collection, Texas Tech University.

Nylander, Chris. Interview by Curtis Peoples, April 16, 2011, tape recording, Oral History Collection, Southwest Collection, Texas Tech University.

Pinkton, Greg. Interview by Monte Monroe, August 16, 2011, tape recording in Oral History Collection, Southwest Collection, Texas Tech University.

Sosebee, Winston. Interview by Paul Carlson, September 27, 2013, notes in possession of author.

Selmon, "Scandalous" John. Interview by Charles Townshend, June 13, 1969, tape recording, Oral History Collection, Southwest Collection, Texas Tech University.

Weaver, Davis. Interview by Curtis Peoples, April 16, 2011, tape recording, Oral History Collection, Southwest Collection, Texas Tech University.

Weaver, Rhonda. Interview by Monte Monroe, April 16, 2011, tape recording, Oral History Collection, Southwest Collection, Texas Tech University.

Wise, Billie Mays. Interview by Curtis Peoples, April 16, 2011, tape recording, Oral History Collection, Southwest Collection, Texas Tech University.

Newspapers

Abilene Reporter-News, 1937–1938, 1950–1955, 1964, 2011.
Anson *Texas Western*, 1890.
Anson *Western Observer*, 1992, 2012.
Buffalo Gap Round Up, 2012.
Bath (Maine) *Daily Times and Weekly Independent*, 1930.
Dallas Morning News, 1891.
Galveston Daily News, 1891.
The Hi-Jester (Anson, Texas, High School), 1922, 1934.
Lubbock Avalanche, 1903.
Lubbock Morning Avalanche, 1924.
Montclair-Glen Ridge Bulletin, 1930.
Nacogdoches *Daily Sentinel*, 2011.
New York Sun, 1883.
The New York Times, 1912, 1934.
The Pittsburgh Press, 1901.
Sulphur Springs, Texas, *Country World*, 2009.
Taylor County News, 1886.
The Western-Enterprise (Anson, Texas), 1933, 1937, 1939.

Books, Articles, and Other Sources

Ainslie, Ricardo C. *No Dancin' in Anson: An American Story of Race and Social Change*. Northvale, NJ: Janson Aronson Inc., 1995.

Aitkin, Jamie. "No Dancin' in Anson." *Texas Monthly* 14, no. 12 (December 1986): 168, 170, 172, 174.

Alderson, Edwin Anderson, Joel Chandler Harris, and Charles William Kent. *Library of Southern Literature*. 16 vols. Atlanta: Martin & Hoyt Company, 1907, 1909.

Allen, Frederick Lewis. *Only Yesterday: An Informal History of the 1920s*. New York: Harper & Row Publishers, 1931. Reprint, 1964.

Aston, B. W., and Donathan Taylor. *Along the Texas Forts Trail*. Denton: University of North Texas Press, 1997.

Barkley, Roy R., et al. *The Handbook of Texas Music*. Austin: Texas State Historical Association, 2003.

Barrett, Leonora. "The Story of Folk Dancing at the Chittenden Cowboys' Christmas Ball." *The Southwest Musician* 10, no. 1 (September–October 1943): 19, 22.

Boatright, Mody C., and Donald Day, eds. *Backwoods to Border*. Texas Folk-Lore Society, Publications, no. 18. Dallas: Southern Methodist University Press, 1943.

Braucher, Scott, and Bette Ramsey, eds., *Buck Ramsey's Grass with Essays on His Life and Work.* Foreword by B. Byron Price. Lubbock: Texas Tech University Press, 2005.

Campbell, Randolph B. *Gone to Texas: A History of the Lone Star State.* New York: Oxford University Press, 2003.

Cannon, Hal, ed. *Rhymes of the Ranges: A New Collection of the Poems of Bruce Kiskaddon.* Salt Lake City: Gibbs M. Smith, Inc., 1987.

Carlson, Paul H. *Empire Builder in the Texas Panhandle: William Henry Bush.* College Station: Texas A & M University Press, 1996.

———. *The Plains Indians.* College Station: Texas A & M University Press, 1998.

Carr, Joe, and Alan Munde. *Prairie Nights and Neon Lights.* Lubbock: Texas Tech University Press, 1997.

Carroll, H. B. "Coronado's Step-Children: Social Life in the Early South Plains." *West Texas Historical Association Year Book* 9 (1933): 60–68.

Casey, Betty. *Dance Across Texas.* Austin: University of Texas Press, 1985.

Chittenden, William Lawrence. *Bermuda Verses.* New York: G. P. Putnam's Sons, 1909.

———. "The Cowboys' Christmas Ball." *The Cattleman* 39, no. 7 (December 1952): 11.

———. *Ranch Verses.* New York: G. P. Putnam's Sons, 1893.

———. *Ranch Verses.* Rev., enl. ed. New York: G. Putnam's Sons, 1898.

Clarke, Mary Whatley. *The Swenson Saga and the SMS Ranches.* Austin, TX: Jenkins Publishing Company, 1976.

Covington, Marilyn, comp. *A Texas Christmas.* Foreword by Janice Woods Windle. Englewood, CO: Westcliffe Publishers, 1999.

"The Cowboys' Christmas Ball," by the Rambling Longhorn. *Farm and Ranch* 55, no. 4 (February 15, 1936): 2—3.

Cox, James. *History and Biographical Record of the Cattle Industry and Cattlemen of Texas and Adjacent Territory.* St. Louis, MO: Woodward and Tiernan Printing Co., 1895.

Cox, Mike. *West Texas Tales.* Charleston, SC: History Press, 2011.

Dale, Edward Everett. *Cow Country.* Norman: University of Oklahoma Press, 1942. Reprint, 1965.

Dary, David. *Cowboy Culture: A Saga of Five Centuries.* New York: Alfred A. Knopf, 1981.

Davidson, Becky. "The Story Behind the Legendary Poem." *Lubbock Magazine* 3, no. 12 (December 1997): 11–12.

———. "Transcending the Moment: Anson's 'The Cowboys' Christmas Ball.' " *West Texas Historical Association Year Book* 78 (2002): 112–26.

Davidson, Paul. " 'Windy Bill' Wilkinson: The real-life legend of the master of the Christmas Ball." *Lubbock Magazine* 3, no. 12 (December 1997): 13.

Denham, Claude, "Frontier Problems and Amusements in Crockett County." *West Texas Historical Association Year Book* 9 (1933): 35–47.

Doty, William G. *Myth: A Handbook.* Westport, CT: Greenwood Press, 2004.

Eagleton, David Foute, ed. *Writers and Writings of Texas.* New York: Broadway Publishing Company, 1913.

Ellis, Kirk. "My, oh, May: The tall tales of Germany's legendary 'Westerner.'" *Roundup Magazine* 20, no. 4 (April 2013): 13–15.

Federal Works Agency. *Cincinnati: A Guide to the Queen City and Its Neighbors.* Cincinnati: Ohio State Archaeological and Historical Society, 1943.

Fife, Austin, and Alta Fife, eds. *Ballads of the Great West*: Palo Alto, CA: American West Company, 1970.

Fischer, David Hackett. *Albion's Seed: Four British Folkways in America.* New York: Oxford University Press, 1989.

Fleming, Lance. "That Lively Gaited Sworray." *The Tomboy Chronicle* 16, no. 11 (November 2003): 87–88, 90.

Gioia, Dana. *Can Poetry Matter? Essays on Poetry and American Culture.* St. Paul, MN: Greywolf Press, 1992.

Gough, Lysius. *Western Travels and Other Rhymes.* Dallas: A. D. Aldridge & Co., 1886.

Grace, Hybernia. "Larry Chittenden and West Texas." *West Texas Historical Association Year Book* 13 (1937): 3–8.

Greene, A. C. *Sketches from the Five States of Texas.* College Station: Texas A & M University Press, 1998.

Harris, Charles W., and Buck Rainey, eds. *The Cowboy: Six-Shooters, Songs, and Sex.* Norman: University of Oklahoma Press, 1976.

Hartman, Gary. *History of Texas Music.* College Station: Texas A & M University Press, 2008.

Hazard, Lucy Lockwood. *The Frontier in American Literature.* New York: Frederick Ungar Publishing Co., 1927. Reprint, 1961.

History of Cincinnati and Hamilton County, Ohio. Cincinnati: S. B. Nelson & Company, 1894.

Hoinski, Michael. "The Drop Everything List." *Texas Monthly* 38, no. 12 (December 2010): 10.

Holden, William Curry. *Alkali Trails or Social and Economic Movements of the Texas Frontier, 1846–1900.* Dallas: Southwest Press, 1930.

Hutto, Homer, and V. Marie Smith, eds. *Jones County Centennial Celebration.* Anson, TX: Western Observer, 1981.

James, Will. *Cow Country.* New York: Charles Scribner's Sons, 1927.

Jordan, Terry G. *North American Cattle-Ranching Frontiers: Origins, Diffusion, and Differentiation.* Albuquerque: University of New Mexico Press, 1993.

Landers, Emmett M. "From Range Cattle to Blooded Stock Farming in the Abilene Country." *West Texas Historical Association Year Book* 9 (1933): 69–81.

"Larry Chittenden and His Autograph Library." *Frontier Times* 11, no. 1 (October 1933): 37–42.

Lee, Katie. "Gail Gardner and the Sierry Petes." *Journal of Arizona History* 15, no. 3 (Autumn 1974): 209–22.

Leuchtenburg, William E. *The Perils of Prosperity, 1914–1932.* Chicago: University of Chicago Press, 1958.

Lomax, John A. *Adventures of a Ballad Hunter.* New York: Macmillian Company, 1947.

———. *Cowboy Songs and Other Frontier Ballads.* Rev. and enl. ed. New York: Sturgis and Walton Company, 1916.

———. *Songs of the Cattle Trail and Cow Camp.* New York: Macmillan Company, 1919. Reprint, 1927.

Lomax, John A., and Alan Lomax. *Cowboy Songs and Other Frontier Ballads.* Rev. and enl. ed. New York: Macmillan Company, 1941.

———. *Folk Song: U. S. A.* New York: Duell, Sloan and Pearce, 1947.

Malone, Bill. *Country Music U. S. A.* 2nd rev. ed. Austin: University of Texas Press, 2008.

Martell, Joanne, comp. *American Christmases: Firsthand Accounts of Holiday Happenings from Early Days to Modern Times.* Winston-Salem, NC: John H. Blair, Publisher, 2005.

McClure, Boone. "Lysius Gough." *Panhandle-Plains Historical Review* 16 (1946): 28–34.

McCombs, Joe S. "On the Cattle Trail and Buffalo Range, Joe S. McCombs." Contributed by Ben O. Grant and J. R. Webb. *West Texas Historical Association Year Book* 11 (1935): 17–32.

McCoy, Joseph G. *Historic Sketches of the Cattle Trade of the West and Southwest.* Lincoln: University of Nebraska Press, 1985.

McDowell, Robert, ed. *Cowboy Poetry Matters, From Abilene to the Mainstream: Contemporary Cowboy Writing.* Ashland, OR: Story Line Press, 2000.

McKay, S. S. "Economic Conditions in Texas in the 1870s." *West Texas Historical Association Year Book* 15 (1939): 84–127.

McKey, Nola. "The Texas Cowboys' Christmas Ball." *Texas Highways* 50, no. 12 (December 2003): 40–45.

Mooar, J. Wright. "The Frontier Experiences of J. Wright Mooar." *West Texas Historical Association Year Book* 4 (1928): 89–92.

Mowry, George E., ed. *The Twenties: Ford, Flappers & Fanatics.* Englewood Cliffs, NJ: Prentice-Hall, Inc., 1963.

Murphey, Michael Martin. "Cowboy Christmas: Anson, Texas Origins to a National Revival: A Brief History and Personal Recollection." *American West Magazine* 1, no. 4 (December 2000–January 2001): 8–9, 11–12.

Murrah, David J. *The Pitchfork Land and Cattle Company: The First Century.* Lubbock: Texas Tech University Press, 1983.

Pace, Robert F., and Donald S. Frazier. *Frontier Texas: History of a Borderland to 1880.* Abilene, TX: State House Press, 2004.

Pinkard, Tommie. "A Lively Sworray." *Texas Highways* 26, no. 12 (December 1979): 8–12.

Powers, Robbie M. "Larry Chittenden—A Bard of the Texas Range," *The Cattleman* 16, no. 7 (December 1929): 15, 17–18.

Rathjen, Frederick W. *The Texas Panhandle Frontier.* Rev. ed. Introduction by Elmer Kelton. Lubbock: Texas Tech University Press, 1998.

Roach, Joyce Gibson, ed. *Texas and Christmas.* 2nd ed. Fort Worth, TX: TCU Press, 2004.

Roberts, Emmett. "Frontier Experiences of Emmett Roberts." *West Texas Historical Association Year Book* 3 (1927): 43–58.

Rogers, Mondel. *Old Ranches of the Texas Plains.* College Station: Texas A & M University Press, 1976.

Rollins, Philip Aston. *The Cowboy: An Unconventional History of Civilization on the Old-Time Cattle Range.* Rev. and enl. ed. Norman: University of Oklahoma Press, 1997.

Russell, Tony. *Country Music Records: A Discography, 1921–1942.* New York: Oxford University Press, 2004.

Sheppard, Jon. "The Texas Cowboys' Christmas Ball." *American West Magazine* 2 (Winter 2002): 8–9.

Shelton, Hooper, and Homer Hutto. *First 100 Years of Jones County, Texas.* Stamford, TX: Shelton Press, 1978.

Skarnulis, Leanna. "Cowboys' Christmas Ball." *American Profile*, December 3, 2009, 14–16.

Spraberry, Doris, ed. *Cowboy Country: The Poetry of Larry Chittenden, The Ranch Poet of West Texas.* Anson: Anson Public Library, 2001.

Stanley, David, and Elaine Thatcher, eds. *Cowboy Poets and Cowboy Poetry.* Urbana: University of Illinois Press, 2000.

TCCB Association. *The Texas Cowboys' Christmas Ball Ranch Supper Cookbook.* Hawley, TX: Texas Cowboys' Christmas Ball Association, 2012.

Texas Almanac, 2006–2007. Dallas: The Dallas Morning News, 2006.

Texas Almanac, 2012–2013. Denton: Texas State Historical Association, 2012.

Thorp, Nathan Howard, "Jack," comp. *Songs of the Cowboys.* Estancia, NM: News Print Shop, 1908.

Tinsley, Jim Bob. *He Was Singin' This Song.* Gainesville: University Press of Florida, 1981.

Tompkins, Charles H. "A Letter About Larry Chittenden's Poem," *The Cattleman* 39, no. 8 (January 1953): 196–97.

Tyler, Ron, et al. *The New Handbook of Texas.* 6 vols. Austin: Texas State Historical Association, 1996.

Webb, Walter Prescott. *The Great Plains.* New York: Grosset & Dunlap, 1931.

White, James T., ed. *The National Cyclopaedia of American Biography.* 63 vols. New York: J. T. White, Co., 1890–1953.

Work, James C., ed. *Prose and Poetry of the American West.* Lincoln: University of Nebraska Press, 1990.

Page numbers in *italics* refer to illustrations.